The Art of Bernard Leach

The Art of Bernard Leach

EDITED BY CAROL HOGBEN

FABER AND FABER

London and Boston

First published in 1978 by
Faber and Faber Ltd
3 Queen Square, London WCI

ISBN 0 571 11291 9

Copyright © 1978 Lund Humphries Publishers Ltd

Created for Faber and Faber Ltd
by Lund Humphries Publishers Ltd
and based on the retrospective exhibition
'The Art of Bernard Leach'
held at the Victoria and Albert Museum, London, in 1977

Designed by Herbert Spencer
Filmset by Keyspools Ltd, Golborne, Lancashire
Printed by Lund Humphries, Bradford, Yorkshire
Colour blocks by Gilchrist Brothers Ltd, Leeds, Yorkshire
Bound by J M Dent & Sons (Letchworth) Ltd

Foreword

Carol Hogben
Regional Services Department,
Victoria and Albert Museum

This book is based on the major retrospective exhibition that was held at the Victoria and Albert Museum in London, at the beginning of 1977, in honour of the artist's ninetieth birthday. Every piece, drawing, or print that is illustrated here, among the plates, was also included in that exhibition – which we tried, within certain limits, to make as representative as possible. It displayed almost two hundred pots with some thirty early prints and later drawings, and was brought together from over seventy sources, both private and public. There was none, however, that came from overseas, and we did not, for example, seek any early pieces in Japan. It was carefully titled 'The Art of Bernard Leach', and was built on unique pieces bearing his personal mark. It did not include any of the standard repetition wares, made at the St Ives Pottery and based on his designs, although many would consider their production the fleet if not the flagship of his fame. It did not include the earliest of his etchings, drawings, and paintings that were made before the first show of his pots. And it has not been possible to reproduce here quite everything that came in our selection.

At the time the exhibition was first planned, we at one point thought of calling it 'Leach – Potter', in compliment to his great book on his friend, which he had simply titled 'Hamada – Potter'. To have thought it, however, even for one instant, was to realise it would not do at all. For in Hamada's case it was summary, precise. Nothing could with any use be added. But Leach falls in a category of his own, where his writings (and, to some extent, his drawings) have been just as important expressions as his pots.

To make this clear, the gallery display included an anthology of extracts that were taken from all his principal prose writings. These were purposely selected not only to tell, *seriatim*, in his own published words, the outline of his personal life-story, but to put on show the development of his thinking in parallel with the development of his art. They were treated on the wall as verbal drawings, and helped to chart the drift of his career. They are now reprinted here by kind permission, both of the author and of the publishers concerned. They are to be regarded, like the plates, as illustrations – the one depicting a sequence of his pots, the other a selection of his thoughts. With the equally kind permission of the owners, the opportunity was taken to photograph the very great majority of exhibits, to make possible this commemorative volume. Colour photographs were taken by Christopher McGlashan, of the Museum's staff; black and white ones were taken, for the Museum, by David Cripps, with a small number by Peter MacDonald, again of the staff. Plate captions have been adapted from the exhibition catalogue (which had little illustration) and were written by David Coachworth of the Museum's Department of Regional Services, with the benefit of extended consultations with David Leach. The bibliography and chronological notes, prepared by John Houston, now similarly reappear as in that catalogue. The piece, however, on 'Leach as Author' by Edwin Mullins, was specially invited for this volume, and we are happy to print it here for the first time.

By the circumstances of its exhibition origin this book appears (and may well long remain) the fullest range available of Leach's work, by illustration, in Western collections, although a comparable volume was published in Japan, in 1966, on the occasion of an earlier retrospective.

Its text, on the other hand, has in every way to recognise that Leach himself is far ahead his own best interpreter, best analyst, apologist, biographer, protagonist. Most readers will probably already have seen those main writings that are currently available in print. It would have been pointless to regurgitate a digest, however thoroughly studied, that merely told his tale in different words. But two short pieces of his that might otherwise have become lost, are put back here on record unabridged, for their documentary value, in an appendix. And I have attempted my own essay of appraisal to try and set down what I personally feel, as a result of having organised that exhibition. It is not meant to instruct or to inform so much as to open a discussion of the artist's future standing, as a prophet of still relevant crafts standards. It is my hope that Bernard Leach will accept this book in public homage. For it is certainly, among other things, so intended. It is my hope that those who saw our show (brilliantly installed, as it was, by Ivor Heal) will accept it as a reasonably adequate reminder of the work. But it is still more my hope that many other readers, not only in this country but elsewhere, who did not have that chance, will find in it a recognisable portrayal of the greatest artist-potter-writer of this age.

March 1978

8

Introduction

Carol Hogben

Where Leach lives now – still in St Ives, no longer at the Pottery – his home is on a wall beside the sea. The sands of a beach come right beneath his window, where the higher tides will actually lap its foot. It faces to the west, and each day ends with the burning ritual drowning of the sun.

The sky is full of seagulls, at all seasons, that are looking for the hidden fish below. The bluffs behind are bare of trees and windy. The riches of the land lie underground in seams, as old spyhole mine-buildings here and there remind. It is a finely elemental sort of place, where water, fire, earth and air continuously test their grip upon each other; and it is a good symbolic habitat for Leach.

For Leach is a man who thinks in primal images, and likes to keep his mind on central themes. About all such he has impassioned stances, and talks with all the gusto of a preacher. To be a potter and so work with one's hands (using wheel, water, clay and draught-fed fire), while at the same time being also an artist, and kneading out the feelings of one's life, is to him a simply blissfully high calling. Conveying as much to the young is one chief mission.

He would like to speak supportively to every craftsman, and lift their belief in the importance of their work. But he also wants to lose the fewest possible moments from urging his most precious of all dreams, which is to tie the East and West in closer understanding. He worries a good deal about The Bomb; gets joy from his faith (he is a Baha'i); quotes Blake; tells Zen crystal enigmatic nuggets; explains the Tao.

He has on the wall of his room the reproduction of a painting by Van Gogh. It speaks to him still just as freshly as it did when he first hung it. And it has not lost one whit of its intensity from being now familiar to the world. Great truths to him stay bright, and keep being felt.

I hope I have not given the impression that Leach is a portentous man to talk to. He loves life, and keeps general good humour. He is a very positive sort of person, with the warmest easy engagement in others' affairs. He has a lively sensibility, and a long stock of pithy reminiscence. He seems entirely lacking mean or unkind thoughts. He likes to be direct and plain in speech.

To look at physically he is a biggish, squarish man, with broad shoulders, and flat, large-fingered hands. His hair is thick, somewhat unruly, not specially white – not snowily at least. He has virtually been blind since 1973. He can still keep up his writing by dictating, but he can no longer see to make a pot. His curiosity about the world has never slackened, and he talks to all his visitors with zest. I cannot believe that any of these leave him without some glow of feeling for his courage.

Everybody knows his most remembered saying, 'The pot is the man . . .', and anyone who wants can check the character I have been trying here to describe against the plates. The key words of his formal critical vocabulary tend to hinge on strength, energy, vigour; on honesty, vitality, weight; generosity; solidity.

Belly curves are robust, necks stately, edges firm. Feet are broad. His glaze colourings, sometimes rich, are never sharp. Generally they are soft, earthy, plain, with any accidental subtleties gratefully accepted. You know he likes to turn things in his hand.

He is a master with the graver and the plane, more, perhaps, than a genius at the wheel. But his rarest artistry, here at least in the west, is his flowing rapid use of brush and trailer. Of the recurrent decorative emblems he has used, many take the forms of daemon energies – the soaring bird in the air, fish in the sea, horse in the field. His well-heads tap the springs of inner earth, his mountainous landscapes frisk their hills at the sky. His oaken trees-of-life, with birds and oxen, exhibit an extraordinary rhythmic strength. His bracken fronds are principles of growth.

In such literary, figurative terms, then, we can see a man who thinks in primal images. And when we look, perhaps, at some of those simpler classic pieces of his that restate the virtues of a Sung Chinese, or Yi Korean, or Mediaeval English model, we see the same man free-thinking on the essences of pottery as art.

It is true that a great deal of his work is plain and simple, yet it speaks to us in an elevated key. One can never somehow mistake but that it is always concerned with goodness, that it makes a statement about how to live in grace – loving people, loving nature, loving clay, loving great non-bombastic works of art, and helping others; always trying to be honest and unassuming, not out to bring a shallow, short effect so much as a long-lasting durable affection; and not being afraid, either, of working on a heightened moral plane; for one can be seriously inclined yet smile at life. I have tried then to suggest, deliberately, that there is a real man called Bernard Howell Leach, who lives in a still visitable real place. He is the very same person as the potter; and if you look at the pictures of his pots, you should be able to check what he is like. They are, after all, not only the whole man in themselves, but whoever keeps any one of them unbroken will also keep a part of him alive. However, I have not yet sketched the time-scale of this picture, or put it in its real global space. For we are certainly talking about an artist of world stature, who was born more than ninety years ago; whose greatest potting work was probably done while in his seventies, yet whose first one-man show was held in Tokyo before the breaking out of World War One; who has personally made, he reckons, over 100,000 pots and whose St Ives Pottery (which of course he founded) has probably turned out something over a million (with all the ownerships which that figure implies); who has had more than a hundred one-man exhibitions, in over a score of countries; the best collection of whose work is shown in Tokyo, not in the Museum of Western Art but among that of his Japanese *confrères*; and who has shared with Hamada a unique act of homage at the Louvre; whose *A Potter's Book* has gone through fifteen English printings, totalling well over 100,000 copies, and has been translated into at least four languages.

We are talking, moreover, about the husband of the potter Janet Leach;

10

Contents

Page 7   Foreword by Carol Hogben

9   Introduction by Carol Hogben

15   Leach as Author by Edwin Mullins

21   Writings

43   Tributes

46   Bernard Leach: Chronology

49   Pots (Illustrations 1–123)

161   Drawings and etchings (Illustrations 124–143)

179   Descriptions of the illustrations

185   Select Bibliography

Two early declarations:

186   A Review 1909–1914 (1914)

189   A Potter's Outlook (1928)

Examples of marks:
(a) painted, 1912 (b) slip, 1923
(c, d) impressed, c.1920–40
(e, f) impressed, c.1940–73

about the father of the potters David and Michael, the grandfather of the potter John Leach; the founder, you might say, of the Leach Dynasty! We are talking about the spiritual elder brother of Shoji Hamada, Kenkichi Tomimoto, and Kanjiro Kawai; the first master of Michael Cardew, Norah Braden, Katherine Pleydell-Bouverie, and a hundred others; about a man who has lectured, worked, and taught around the world, and whose two film portraits on television, from years back, are still regularly revived; about a man whose direct preaching words have given, I would guess, at least a thousand young people, especially in America, the courage to make their livelihood as potters.

And all these people, whose lives he has really affected, mingle some part of his values with their own, and clear their debt by passing it to others.

The point I am trying to make then is that *this* person (who is also that same potter) is not an ageing man, sitting there in St Ives, with a long life nine parts spent. He is someone rather who belongs to all of us, with a long future ahead of him; whose pots will be seen, whose books will be read, and whose tales will be told for at least another whole generation foreseeably to come, in more parts of the world than he ever visited himself. Moreover, new evaluations lie ahead that have not yet been made, and new tests should be considered for his relevance. For it is only just beginning to be possible to weigh the line of his life as a single whole, without imposing any false consistency. Indeed, this present book is meant to be a step in that direction.

There is room, of course, for an infinite number of opinions as to who is the *finest* potter of our age. But there cannot be two views as to which has had the greatest influence on others. There just has not been any other book, by any other potter, of any other place in time or country, that can match the currency of Leach's *A Potter's Book*.

I realise, of course, that not everyone nowadays thinks that the sheer continuance of that influence is for the good. At least one English critic, who may speak for many, considers it a sort of dreadful malign cloud, distorting our enjoyment of industrial pots, and making it generally almost impossible for a renaissance of porcelain to serve the people, free to be both frivolous and witty, free to be brightly coloured and elaborate, free to be sculptural, perhaps. To use dull, unmagic, repeating things like moulds; to be individualistic, self-conscious, self-observant, without feeling The Master's disapproval.

There are points to answer here in just a moment. But if this is the sort of attack that is made on Leach's long-taken positions by a hostile critic popping off out front, he is probably hit more seriously from the rear where far too many imitative supporters have insufficient talent for the game. The sight of an apparently thriving crafts shop – it could even be in a back-lane of tourist-overrun St Ives itself in summer – filled with drear, lifeless copies of copies of copies, can be deeply depressing, enough in fact to put one off for ever. And yet, then, round another corner, perhaps in the Penwith Gallery, say, one comes across a sight of the real thing, and one's confidence is immediately restored. It is possible to think that the conditions of Leach's youth are gone for good, and that any message based on his experience is bound, today, to fall well short of the mark. The potatoes Raleigh brought back from America are now a part of all the Old World's diet, and no one longer looks for seed crops there, particularly. Similarly no one needs ever again to feel that one has to go back all the way to Japan to get the first-hand nourishment Leach found there.

Yet it still remains the case, as Leach wrote in 1914, that the only valid reason for studying the art of the past was for him to gain confidence in studying the present. The fact that he personally found it, living in Japan, from Chinese art of the Sung Dynasty, is not the true essential of the matter – which is that he found it with his own personal eye. It is important always to remember clearly that his range of touchstone standards crossed the world. It took in favourite areas of pottery from Persia, Egypt, Africa, Peru, Mexico, Turkey, Mesopotamia, Greece, Italy, Spain, Germany, and England – among others! One does not have to accept his every taste precisely, although he does explain a coherent base for responding. The truth they offer added all together is that pottery is a noble ancient art, the wide world over, and that those are happiest who make their pots today in a sense of adding something to that art. No one, before Leach, ever put this one-world one-art message quite so clearly. Just so, again, the fact that he met a living peasant school of country potters, continuing on from father to son, while in Japan, and was able to learn from it, is not necessarily the essential of that matter. I fancy it is rather that he learned to watch their ways, and then went on to make his own mistakes. By building his own kiln, digging his own clay (to eye and not to formula) and sieving his own wood ashes, he acquired an unshakeable confidence in having his command, and meeting any accidents that came. Getting a practical mastery of process for oneself is not a message less relevant today. And confidence is still what every artist needs. The precise way he learnt it is not crucial.

So then one comes to such other important questions as how the hand-craftsman is going to justify his chosen way of life in an industrial society. It is a black mark on Leach's preaching record that he talked of industry as if it were Belial, its workshops a place for merely mindless slaves. But I personally assume this blindness to have been wilful. Committed to his private independence, he did not want to think that any other ways were really possible. Or so it would seem he used at least to talk. In practice though his pottery grew at times very close to being like a small industrial unit. Certainly he faced the questions of making useful repetitive wares by old hand methods a good deal more thoroughly than most of his fellow craftsmen of the day, within the market context that they knew. And what he seems successfully to have brought here from Japan and introduced to Britons was not so much a matter of oriental glazes, or the actual complete ceremony of tea, so much as a rumour of it, a whiff as you might say. He just somehow seemed to convey that hand-made potters' pots, in the firing of which is still a part for hazard, are necessarily and long-lastingly more interesting to hold than any merely factory-turned-out vessel.

The Leach solution of having a small workshop that was founded on a core of repetition, but that kept good place for creative unique pieces, paid off twice over. Although it might not have seemed so at the time, it was later clear that he had gained a tremendous deal from being personally involved in that useful repetition. He learned from it the deepest meaning of being economical, and of lucidity; and it gave the shop a unifying purpose. In the end the most important thing of all, however, was that he could use this workshop base to draw away, and devote the later years of his life to a perfected and a purer private art. It had taught him some of the problems of being a craftsman, and it let him return an artist better equipped.

I spoke before of Leach's art developing. And we will not have understood him at all unless we see some changes in his ground. One must never forget that Leach came into pottery from fine art. His first studies were painting, drawing, etching. He always, therefore, knew himself as an artist who had freely chosen a craft as his expression. It is not so easy a kind of faith to get, and were harder had it been the other way around.

It was natural, at the beginning, to assume that fine art trends had relevance for crafts, and that post-impressionism, for example, must point out ways ahead for younger potters. Later in his life he watched the painting scene in general less intently (although immediately being won, at Dartington, to Mark Tobey), but in early days the force of Van Gogh's drawings and his colour was quick to have effect on Leach's work, as etcher-potter. So he started out, we see, a thoroughly loose-bridled, Blake-inspired romantic, with plenty of self and feelings on the line. It was only very much later, back in England, that he would begin to argue intellectually to himself the importance of such concepts as non-being, and deride individual expression as feeble indulgence. But the thing we have to notice is that his own pots, the unique ones at least picked out for exhibition, are not successful proofs of these beliefs, and the strength of his personal vision is always toweringly clear even when, apparently, his forms are their most classical.

What I am saying by this not least is in effect that the potter and the preacher in him sometimes diverge. The potter does not absolutely practice what the preacher preaches. He pots out of his soul. He writes with the Welsh preachers' *hwyl*. If ever the two statements do not match, I would always follow the pots and not the words.

Over and over again one comes back to the baseline confidence of his self-taught, well experienced, quick-responding eye. He tells us of the batch of twenty pots that are all exactly the same, the one made in the same way as the other. Yet you can look at them and tell that only one has life; the rest have nothing. The parable is true. We may believe it. And it entitles us to look at all his work in just this spirit. Leach's own spirit is always positive. It does put faith in personal humane values, and it keeps their standard by to use as test. As long as the next directions for the crafts are ever discussed, that test, and his unified art vision, are always going to be there and have their relevance. But the idea that his influence should be felt oppressive, by anyone, is quite absurd. We do not have to keep his every text as gospel, though it were good to remember what he actually said. We only have to keep what still inspires us. We are free to reject whatever does not help. We should recognise he sometimes changed his mind, wisely enough. He tried all kinds of bodies for his pots, and an exceptional range of decorative techniques. He may seem at some times to have taken a strong stand against, for example, such things as moulds and yet to have used them. He has tried, rather improbably, enamel painting on others' porcelain blanks, for sheer fun. Above all, when it comes to the point, he has loved every minute of his working life, and he has fulfilled Yanagi's prophecy of 1920, that he would make eternal masterpieces one day, many times over. It is a legacy that begs us to enjoy it, with a light heart, and an open feeling mind.

Chess set, porcellaneous stoneware.
Made at St Ives, 1939.
Collection: Mr Theyre Lee-Elliott

Leach as Author

Edwin Mullins

A Potter's Book came out in May 1940: hardly the moment, one would have thought, for converting the British to the joy of clay and glazes. Nonetheless it sold out, ran into a second edition right after the war, and is now in its fifteenth. For thirty-eight years it has remained *the* book on how to make pots; and through it Leach has undoubtedly found an audience far wider than the public with direct access to his work as a potter. Since 1940 there have been plenty of potters who have rejected much of Leach's craft philosophy, and who have declined to follow in his footsteps; but it is fair to suggest that they might not have been potters at all but for Leach. And how many of them, I wonder, have not at some time or other found *A Potter's Book* a mine of wisdom and know-how, and as a result of reading it have not been compelled to think more deeply about the craft they practise?

It is rare to find a successful artist – or indeed a man successful in any field – who is prepared to be entirely open about what he does. Most men at the top are jealous of being overtaken, or they enshrine their success in professional mystique, or perhaps sense the threat of exposure if they are quite honest. Not Leach. *A Potter's Book* guards no trade secrets. His kilns collapse and he tells about it so that we may avoid the same mistakes. He does not always like his own work and says so. The week's takings drop to £8 (Leach was already middle-aged) and he makes it clear this sort of thing is liable to happen if you venture on such a lonely path. The one thing he never does is stand aloof or in contempt of fellow-potters. It was Georges Braque – in so many ways the humblest of artists – who wrote 'Those who lead have their backs turned to those who follow, which is what those who follow deserve'. A neat jibe; but Leach would never have said that. Nowhere in his writings is there a hint of false pride in being a pioneer. *A Potter's Book* is dedicated 'to all potters'. His books radiate an excitement of discovery, as if he can scarcely wait to share those discoveries. If ever a man was the sum of his enthusiasms, it is Bernard Leach.

He is, of course, a born observer, and a born *raconteur*. In a later book, *A Potter in Japan* (1960), Leach describes with wry pleasure his friend Yanagi pointing out that Keats's 'Ode to a Grecian Urn' was very likely composed in honour of a very bad pot. And to be fêted in Japan, where Leach has spent so much of his life, may be very gratifying for an artist, and it is a privilege indeed to be offered a hotel-room last occupied by the Emperor – until you are woken at 6.30 in the morning by twittering women determined to see where their revered Emperor slept.

A Potter in Japan is a delight and deserves to be reprinted. On one level it is the diary of a man's return to live for two years in a country he has loved; only now, instead of the almost medieval Japan he once knew, he tries to come to terms with a nation smashed by the atomic bomb, many of its social and artistic values pulverised, its streets patrolled by G.I.'s and ringing with pop-music, and its new leaders hell-bent on creating the most efficient industrial super-power of the mid-twentieth century. On a more intimate level it is a book about the Japanese themselves, in particular the artists and craftsmen and men of culture, and their efforts to resist or adjust to change as they stand uneasily with one foot in the old Japan and one in the new. And on another level still it is a book about the West, about Western culture seen from the viewpoint of the author who is himself endeavouring to make that adjustment between East and West, between old and new, between the quiet values of the Tea Ceremony and the rowdy demands of a jet-age. How does a man of sensibility sail straight in this sea of so many tides, how does he find his true self and the standards by which he lives, and where can he make his most valuable contribution?

These are issues which have occupied Leach all his working life. Here is the complex intellectual matrix – a search for standards, a search for faith – which has cherished and given shape to so humble and unintellectual a thing, a pot. A mere pot, we might have said before Leach arrived on the scene. 'Very few people in this country think of the making of pottery as an art . . .' are the opening words of *A Potter's Book*. But 'pots . . . are human expressions', of special value to a world in which, Leach points out, we can now produce more or less whatever we need but most of what we make is inhuman; for 'the sheer technique of living has overwhelmed life itself' and 'we may hope to find in good pots those innate qualities which we most admire in people'.

This synthesis of the inner man and the environment he creates is the root of Leach's working philosophy, and from it grow the humanity and infectious enthusiasm which characterise the way he writes about his craft. Activities that to a layman may sound humdrum enough – like pulling the handle of a jug, or packing a kiln, or prospecting the Cornish landscape for suitable clay – become a human adventure we are invited to share: matters of significance. Or, again, Leach being introduced to raku-glaze potting at a party in Tokyo in 1911, where for him it all began: that too becomes an adventure and a revelation. On a much later visit to the East Leach is told of more than one hundred pots which have turned up in a country district of Japan (*Kenzan*, 1966). Could these be long-lost work by the first Kenzan made 250 years ago? Leach describes the find and the controversy surrounding it with the excitement many of us experienced in the West when a lost notebook of Leonardo da Vinci turned up in Spain a few years ago.

All Leach's writing is enriched by this sense of relish. The joy of making pots embraces everything connected with them: the soil and landscape from which the clay and glazes come, nature which supplies the decorative motifs, food and drink and flowers with which pots are intimately associated, and the people themselves who make pots and for whose domestic lives they are made. How appropriate that the secret of slipware decoration should have been re-discovered at Leach's St Ives Pottery in the early days by observing what happened when you cut through a thick slice of bread and jam which had been laden with Cornish cream!

Leach's ideal has always been that the human hand should be the ally of the machine, not its enemy. 'I would have liked', he writes in *A Potter's Work* (1967), 'to have designed tea-sets and table ware for the English public, and envy Josiah Wedgwood that privilege, but I would have had to own a factory, and I had neither the talent, the desire nor the money to do this.' Here in a nutshell lies the predicament not just of Leach himself but of all craftsmen and creative designers who have wished to make an impact on the industrial scene and could only hope to do so by forfeiting the creative independence essential to them. William Morris, perhaps, came closest to achieving the impossible. Leach himself cites the American furniture-designer Charles Eames, as well as some modern Danish designers, who he feels have managed a balance between hand and machine in our own day. Elsewhere the scene has looked bleak. In *A Potter's Book* he is writing at a moment in time when, he says, there has been an almost entire loss of our own birthright of traditional craft lore. The result? On the one hand industrial pottery which is generally terrible in form and decoration, due to a 'general lowering of taste under conditions of competitive industrialism'; and on the other hand the unavoidable conclusion that 'no other age has produced such ill-begotten crafts' (*The Potter's Challenge*, 1976).

Into this morass of mediocrity, machine-work and hand-work alike, Leach arrived in 1920 after eleven years in Japan. He had learnt his craft and his outlook from traditional masters working in a country only recently opened up to the outside world, where industrialisation had not yet achieved a stranglehold, and where traditions of craft, though already overlooked, at least still survived. The England to which he returned had long ago led an Industrial Revolution, achieving immense material prosperity as a result, but in the process had virtually starved out its cottage industries and the traditions of hand-skill and design they practised. Leach arrived on the scene as the last 'peasant' potteries were going out.

According to what criteria, then, should he work? The only living traditions at his disposal were from the other side of the globe. Here in England the tradition of slipware was dead; there were merely pieces inside museum glass-cases or in junk-shops. Not surprisingly the experience of founding a pottery in this country became associated with the crucial question of *standards*. Rarely in Leach writings does he stray long from what is to him the central issue, the craftsman's need to relate his activities to some acknowledged ancestry; for '... without standards we are lost, and when the standards are too private, as with us now, we are confused' (*A Potter in Japan*).

As a practising potter Leach's own standards have for the most part been Oriental; not so much Japanese pottery as the classical Korean and Chinese ceramics upon which the Japanese traditions were founded. Since these represent for Leach the pinnacle of the potter's art, and nothing in Europe exists to match them, he felt it natural and right to seek in the perfection of Chinese and Korean pottery the criteria against which to measure his own achievement. In his writings Leach refers to this need over and over again. These oriental leanings have landed him in a packet of trouble among craftsmen suspicious of what they have felt to be the irrelevant emulation of an alien culture. Leach has articulated his own position very clearly: it is basically that you do not have to copy what you hold to be the best. Perhaps the clearest defence of Leach's orientalism came from his first pupil, Michael Cardew, who pointed out that in most ages the significant achievements in European ceramics have been made by men who looked to the Chinese as their masters; which is unanswerable.

Leach's orientalism is not a consciously acquired outlook. Leach is a natural child of the East. He was born there, spent almost half his childhood and early manhood there, has developed his closest working friendships among oriental craftsmen and connoisseurs, and feels himself to be indigenously a man of two cultures. His lifelong friend Soetsu Yanagi, whose writings on aesthetics Leach has adapted into English (*The Unknown Craftsman*, 1972), wrote of Leach that it was 'doubtful whether any other visitor from the West ever shared our spiritual life so completely'. What he shared, and what has sustained him, was the continuity of the living Japanese tradition. It was this that gave meaning and form to the craft he strove to master. When eventually he returned to this country and settled in St Ives, the three-chambered kiln he used was constructed by a Japanese who was a member of the thirty-ninth generation of potters from a Japanese craft village. It was this kind of tradition which Leach found sadly absent in this country, and which he felt the need to import. It was not a matter of copying alien styles but of finding and sharing a common spirit.

An important question must be to what extent Leach has succeeded in building a bridge between two distant cultures, Oriental and European. Broadly speaking the artistic tradition of the Far East has been of reduction and synthesis, that of Europe one of expansion and inquiry. A pot is important in Japan because it is a kind of microcosm: it stands for nature, for human life and relationships, for simple unity. Whereas in Europe a pot is a pot merely, a pot to put things in, an artefact: it may be decorative but is of little spiritual significance, and great art is something quite different.

Leach's natural bent is towards synthesis, and the deepest perceptions contained in his writings are reserved for artists from the East whose work achieves that synthesis in greater measure than, one senses, Leach sometimes feels he has achieved himself. His admiration for his old pupil, Shoji Hamada, of whom he has written an admirable 'working portrait' (*Hamada: Potter*, 1975), is perhaps the outstanding example of his capacity for insight and fellow-feeling. Hamada was for Leach the epitome of the 'unknown craftsman': the man of clear mind and simple faith who chose to work in a traditional Japanese pottery village in Japan, refusing to sign his work. I am reminded of an aphorism uttered by another Japanese potter and quoted by Hamada, that the frog in the well does not know the great ocean but he does know heaven.

And yet Hamada became a national hero in Japan, and his work is sought everywhere where pots are valued. He grew to be famous, in the way that any successful artist in the West is famous. Here is the irony of a living tradition, that outside forces may overtake it as surely as the Whisky-Bar is replacing the Tea Ceremony. Mr Leach is right; it was Tom, Dick and Harry who built Chartres. What he does not say is that, had Chartres been built only yesterday Tom, Dick and Harry would now be travelling the American lecture circuit. It seems to me that implicit in Bernard Leach's writings is the willingness to accept this change and to work with it. 'Modern man finds himself alone in his individualism', he writes: yes, but not as alone as the man who tries to bury his individualism in traditions that willy-nilly have decayed around him. Leach knows this, as of course did Hamada. Both craftsmen have succeeded in building that bridge between East and West by being prepared to seize the best that both worlds have to offer, while managing to keep their personal integrity intact.

March 1978

Beyond East and West, which was published as this book went to press, is not included in this survey of Leach's writings.

Grave cover, of painted stoneware tiles, for the painter Alfred Wallis in St Ives cemetery. Made at St Ives, 1942.

Writings

Leach in his kiln and workshop at
Abiko, Japan in 1917, before the
disastrous fire.

After the fire, the kiln was rebuilt
by Viscount Kouroda, seen here (centre)
in a group including Leach.

Japan 1908–13

Bernard Leach

Extracts from
Looking Backwards and Forwards at 72,
BBC broadcast talk, London, 1959

I did not start life as a potter but as an artist. From childhood I enjoyed drawing more than anything else and so at sixteen when my father asked me what I wanted to be there was no hesitation in my reply. My answer rather dismayed him but my teachers at Beaumont backed me up and rather by chance I presently found myself the youngest student at the Slade School of Art under the famous Henry Tonks. A year or so later my father died and to carry out a death-bed promise to him I tried to become a banker in the Hongkong & Shanghai Bank and very soon came to the conclusion that I was not cut out for that sort of life. Much against the wishes of my family, I returned to art. Then I fell in with the writing of Lafcadio Hearn which reawakened my childhood memories of Hong Kong, where I was born, and of Japan where I had spent the first four years of my life. I became more and more attracted by the Far East, and in 1909, at the age of 22, I went out to Tokyo with the intention of trying to understand the life and art furthest removed from our own.

I had hoped to earn a living by teaching etching which I had studied under Frank Brangwyn. Fortunately for me the skill of my first students was such that I began to question my own idea of teaching in favour of learning and, as I was told years later, it was this change of heart which caused my new found friends to open the doors of Eastern art to me.

I built a Japanese house. I married a cousin, the circle of friendship grew, then one day in 1911 I was invited out to a party of painters, poets, and actors, at which the main entertainment consisted in painting on unglazed biscuit-ware pots which were then and there glazed and fired in a portable 'Raku' kiln. The sight of our pots being taken with long iron tongs, red hot from the charcoal fired muffle chamber, and gradually cooling on tiles until, with cries of excitement, we could handle what we had painted but an hour earlier, awoke in me something dormant and I decided on the spot that I must find a master in this craft. Eventually I was introduced to the 6th Kenzan and he agreed to take me as his pupil.

He was a man of kind and honest character – a craftsman working in a tradition 250 years old rather than an artist of originality like the first and most famous Kenzan. I never attempted to work in my master's style, I felt it would be false for me, a foreigner, to do so.

After about a year he said it was time for me to start on my own and he made a kiln for me in a corner of my garden and eventually gave me a signed 'Densho' or inheritance of the Kenzan title.

Japan 1908–14

Bernard Leach

Extracts from
A Review 1909–1914,
privately published as supplement to a
one-man exhibition of his pots and
etchings, Tokyo, 1914

The complete piece appears as an
appendix at the end of this volume

Six years ago my friend, the artist Henry Lamb, asked me why I was going to Japan.

I was unable to give an answer which satisfied him. Looking back however I do not for one moment regret the step. For not only must anyone who is free to build his own life always be ready to follow an idea which his best friends discourage, and which he himself may be unable to explain, but he may be quite sure that such faithful following of intuition, though it may lead him into unforeseen and even difficult positions, will yet both satisfy his inner needs and also provide him with sufficient material experience with which to build higher. It is not enough for an artist to belong to the present, still less merely to reflect and repeat the past, however remote and exquisite; he must also be an innovator. Searching the past and present for his own soul he must build. All actions are the materialization of ideas, and the finest ideas are mysterious inspirations.

Only now, after nearly six years, am I becoming ready to enjoy old Chinese and Japanese art with a feeling of security. During that time I have studied contemporary art through and with progressive Japanese artists.

Impressionism, Post-Impressionism and the later movements have come to me through their exhibitions and their friendship. I am grateful, for it has saved me from a great danger of being hopelessly lost in the pursuit of ideas, however beautiful, made for and by people of another epoch.

Another point gained is that the study of ancient art and craft which I have made, though limited, has been made from the right angle, that is from the point of view of living art – from the present.

I do not wish to paint what I see, but what I feel through the sense of sight and what I imagine. The matter of the profoundest interest to me is to discover *how* to organise the colour and form of objects so as to produce that feeling, so as to suit the material and space in hand, and yet preserve organic character. This *how* must be a credo of life as well as of art. Its component elements must be united by love.

I should wish to take away men's breath with the wonder of my work, but instead they sit and smile and say it is beautiful! What have I to do with beauty? I want that plough-share force that cut worms hate and forgive, a share of that primitive energy which created the world.

Japan 1920

Soetsu Yanagi

Extract from
An English Artist in Japan,
privately printed in Tokyo, 1920

A fuller and edited version of this piece
appears in *Beyond East and West*

I persuaded him to come to Abiko and set up a kiln there . . . He was full
of hope about his new work, and towards the end of 1916 arrived in
Tokyo with his family. After a good deal of preparation he built his first
kiln at Abiko in the following spring, and adjoining it he constructed a
pretty little workroom of his own design . . .

On the twenty sixth of May of this year 1919 he had finished firing his
eleventh kiln, and was sleeping soundly as usual after the effects of the
necessary vigil, when entirely without ourselves or the village folk
knowing anything about it, his workroom quietly burnt itself out
during the night. Someone came and knocked at our door early in the
morning and surprised us by calling out 'Mr. Leach's house is gone!' and
we ran out to where the building was, but there was nothing left,
nothing but the still heated kiln, just as he had left it, standing under the
burnt-out roof. All his notes that could not be replaced, on the mixture
of earths and glazes, all the rough jottings of the many experiments he
had made, all the labour of many years, in fact, besides numberless
drawings and many volumes of precious books, not to mention
unglazed pots and various potter's tools together with many fine pieces
that he had meant to exhibit a week later – all destroyed leaving hardly a
trace!

Leach came running out after us, aroused by the cry of 'fire', and when
the sudden shock of the sight struck his eyes he stood as if turned to
stone. His face grew pale as he gazed at it. Even now, as the scene of that
moment rises again before my eyes, I have no words to describe it. And
that day, as he sat dejectedly in his chair doing nothing but reflect on his
loss, it was really a sight to move anyone to sympathy. 'What shall I do
now?' he asked me in a dispirited voice. That was a day of silence for all
of us. Leach's face did not light up again until he opened the kiln in
which was the rest of his pottery, and I can only be thankful even now,
both for him and ourselves, that this last kiln was such an unqualified
success, for it raised his spirits again. And a great success, too, awaited
him at the exhibition of this work, and of the furniture designed by him,
which was held soon afterwards.

St Ives 1920

Bernard Leach

Extract from
Hamada-Potter
by Bernard Leach,
published by Kodansha International,
Tokyo, New York, San Francisco, 1975

We began to look around for the two things that potters need most, clay and wood, or fuel.

Taking field-glasses, we began walking round the countryside spying out the land, hoping that we might see a cutting and so find a bed of clay. One day, from a high point known as Trencrom, across the valley we espied a streak of yellowish looking clay in a cutting behind a village called St Erth. We made our way down to the station there, and outside the station on the road there was some clay that had been dropped from a cart. I picked it up. It looked like a yellowish beach sand, but it was plastic, and I had never seen a plastic sand before. This was rather curious. We went into the village and found the foreman of a small clay-digging company, who told us about it. He said that this sandy clay was used as a moulding material for casting bronze, but, also, that at one time in the past he had dug up a very smooth plastic variety in church land nearby. So we went to see the parson, who at that time only asked a price of ten shillings a ton. The clay was about six to eight feet below the surface, and, having the permission to dig, within a week we had some samples...

We had not got our pottery yet, we had not even decided the site. There were several available, and we chose one on the road that is called the Stennack, leading uphill out of St Ives to Land's End. It was a strip of land about one hundred yards long and perhaps twenty or thirty yards wide next to the stream of the same name, the Stennack, which means 'tin stream'

...It struck me one day that in those woods there were a lot of black pines that had died after about thirty years of growth. They were rather inaccessible because of the denseness of the rhododendron undergrowth, which could also be used as fuel. Could I not make an offer to the Great Western Railway to whom it belonged and get a price quotation that was feasible? I did and they sent a man down; we went out and marked the trees and for twenty pounds got all the dead wood. I was rather cunning about it, I think. I realized that the preliminary cutting of paths through the rhododendron to those dead trees produced a lot more wood, so that eventually for twenty pounds we had bought about two hundred tons, and it would cost us about one hundred pounds to get it to the pottery. The whole one hundred yards of our land at the edge of the road was piled with heaps and heaps of mainly rhododendron wood which lasted us, I think, at least two years, perhaps three. So that is how we started with wood, though rhododendron was only partly suitable because it was twisted, which made it difficult to feed into the side of the big kiln, but it was excellent for the stoking of the smaller biscuit and raku kiln.

St Ives 1920–23

Shoji Hamada

Extracts from
Hamada-Potter
by Bernard Leach,
published by Kodansha International,
Tokyo, New York, San Francisco, 1975

On fine days the birds would flock to the fields and break up the soil while feeding on the herring fertilizer. When we saw the birds, we went out to the field nearby and gathered many shards of old pottery from the broken soil. This pottery was the same kind of slipware I had seen at the neighbour's house. From the number of these pieces we concluded that the ware was once used extensively. Studying these fragments, we gathered that the original shapes were circular or rectangles with rounded corners, and that a mould instead of a wheel was used. Diameters ranged from about eight to twenty inches. The larger ones had notched rims, probably for strength.

Picking up the fragments and carefully scrutinizing them, we discovered bands of white clay laid one after another in black clay ground. The effect was similar to inlay, but it is impossible to arrange inlay so widely and flatly. Some fragments contained lines of feathered patterns, while others had simple white patterns in the blackish clay. The colour of the glaze appeared yellow; the red clay body was coated with black slip. In cross section, the white did not simply lie on the surface, but penetrated deeply, as in inlay. Galena glaze was applied only on the inside, and the firing temperature was relatively low. We thought there must be a way to reproduce this method and tried many times, but always missed the mark.

Time passed quickly. My second autumn in St Ives arrived. Blackberries began to ripen in the hedges, and we made blackberry jam. One tea time, we buttered bread, spread on jam, and then covered the jam with thick Cornish clotted cream. I had just cut through these layers, when I happened to glance down, and cried out, 'This is it! This is it! The slipware!' The knife had left patterns like those on slipware through the layers of cream, jam, and butter. I looked at Leach, and he nodded. We rushed to the workshop, leaving the sandwiches uneaten, and tried our new discovery. Never mind tea time. It worked, beautifully! The mysteries of slipware decoration were solved at one try! How interesting that a technique should be discovered in such a natural way. From food to potting. We were able to apply what we saw directly to our problem. It was a good feeling.

St Ives 1920–23

Bernard Leach

Extracts from
Hamada-Potter
by Bernard Leach,
published by Kodansha International,
Tokyo, New York, San Francisco, 1975

In the workshop it was very quiet; over meals, especially supper, we would talk and relax and discuss all aspects of potting – what it meant to be a thinking artist-potter of today, in contrast to the potters of most epochs of the past all over the world; part of a group that produced things scarcely thought about as art for its own sake but considered as enjoyable, right things for normal daily use. I was trained in art; Hamada in pottery technology. We were not folk potters, nor were we simple country folk, like those who made the best English medieval pots (or their counterparts in the Far East) – we were artist-potters and, as such, our horizons had begun to be all horizons. We endlessly discussed all aspects of potting, and we admired what is in folk art and nowhere else.

Coming from the East, Hamada's East, we were on the lookout for quality in a sense that was not recognized in England at that time – it was seen as failure, as bad material. Hardness, whiteness, and translucency were looked upon as the ideal. We brought from the East, Hamada and I, a new concept of quality in pots – of textures, of quiet colours.

We were applying to pots an appreciation of nature, of the natural effects of raw materials.

The general reaction was that our work was dull; the European could not distinguish between one brown and another, or between one texture and another. However, ideas were changing – old Chinese tombs were being excavated, and for the first time work from the Sung dynasty was being seen. The Sung pots, mainly stoneware, were like remelted rock, full of impurities and very close to nature. Their gentle colours and warm textures were a far cry from the decorated porcelains of Staffordshire and Derby.

St Ives 1920–46

Bernard Leach

Extracts from
The Leach Pottery, 1920–46,
published by the
Berkeley Galleries, London, 1946

A fuller and edited version of this piece
appears in *Beyond East and West*

The conclusion we subsequently came to was that making and planning round the individuality of the artist was a necessary step in the evolution of the crafts. So at St Ives, at the outset, we based our economics on the studio and not on the country workshop or the factory.

Hamada and I regarded ourselves as being on the same basis as Murray in London, Decoeur in Paris and Tomimoto in Japan.

For some years our main revenue came from enthusiasts and collectors in London and Tokyo. We worked hard, but with the irregularity of mood. We destroyed pots, as artists do paintings and drawings, when they exhibited shortcomings to our own eyes (what Hamada called 'tail'). We only turned out 2,000 to 3,000 pots a year between four or five of us and of these not more than 10 per cent passed muster for shows. Kiln losses in those days were high – quite 20 per cent. The best pots had to be fairly expensive. What was left over was either sold here or went out on that usually unsatisfactory arrangement of 'sale or return' to Craft Shops up and down the country. Nevertheless our work became known, students arrived, critics were kind, my Japanese friends held repeated exhibitions of my pots and drawings and sent all the proceeds to help establish this pottery in my own country. Neither Hamada nor I, nor Edmund Skinner our first Secretary, ever took more than £100 a year and George Dunn, our clay-worker and wood-cutter, to within a year of his death was easily the best paid at unskilled rates. Without private funds, however, and help from Leonard and Dorothy Elmhirst, we would not have reached security. Strange as it may seem that only came with the close of the war.

Leach visiting the Truro Pottery
with his sons and Hamada, 1923.

St Ives 1928

Bernard Leach

Extracts from
A Potter's Outlook –
Handworkers Pamphlets No. 3
published by New Handworkers'
Gallery, London, 1928

The complete piece appears as an
appendix at the end of this volume

Since 1920, Hamada, Michael Cardew and I have revived the technique of the 17th Century slipware potter. Cardew and I have tried moreover to provide sound hand-made pots sufficiently inexpensive for people of moderate means to take into daily use. But my own experience has taught me that however much this ware expressed the English national temperament of one or two hundred years ago, it does not fit in with modern life.

We cannot forego those other qualifications, of thinness, hardness, non-porosity, and light toned colour.

I then determined to see how far I could succeed in making semi-porcelaineous stoneware. I have reason for a belief that under favourable conditions it is possible to make household pottery with some of the qualities of the 'Sung' or 'T'ang' wares of China. Such pots would satisfy the finer taste and the practical needs of today.

The outward changes I am making in my Pottery are very gradual for any sudden alteration of equipment to a mechanical basis is out of the question. Each power-driven device for saving monotonous human effort has to be tested not only, as in the Industrial world, for efficiency, but also for what I have called its artistic faithfulness.

Actually, my first steps have been to begin with a change from wood to oil-firing, and from hand-grinding to power-grinding, and I shall not hesitate to put in an electrically-driven potter's wheel as soon as I can find a silent and efficient one. When it comes to the question of multiplying production, the complexity increases. I have not gone further than to have tiles made in quantity by semi-mechanical means, thereby halving the price, and to devote the time saved in wood-cutting, grinding, etc. to the reduplication of the more useful stoneware jugs, vases, bowls, etc. by the old hand processes.

St Ives 1931

Bernard Leach

Extract from
Hamada–Potter
by Bernard Leach,
published by Kodansha International,
Tokyo, New York, San Francisco, 1975

Let me now turn to an ash glaze we used. Kenkichi Tomimoto had translated from the Chinese a seventeenth- or eighteenth-century document describing the use of bracken ash glaze for porcelaineous wares. One autumn day some of us were climbing the slopes of Rosewall, the first of a series of rolling hills between us and Land's End, and noticed that the slopes were covered with bracken shoulder high and as brown as the tobacco in a smoker's pouch. It must have been a good year, because the bracken did not always grow so profusely. A few days later we foregathered and cut great amounts of bracken and piled it on clean ground. We burned it slowly, using a watering can to keep it from burning too quickly into a white ash, since we wanted to retain a quantity of black carbon in it to produce a black, or blackish, ash and consequently a reduced effect in the glaze when fired. We had to leave the burning pile overnight, since it was still glowing. Next morning it was cool enough to gather into gunny bags and take down to the pottery. After washing and sieving it, we mixed it with feldspar and, I think, quartz. It made a creamy white, big-crackled glaze, which we have never since equalled. It was velvety white, it took pigment on its surface with gentleness, it did not look mechanized, it was hard and it was soft at the same time. We attempted that same effect in successive years, but never got it again. The reason for this was partly the season in which the dried vegetable was taken from the hills, and partly, no doubt, the amount of salt in the sea air that had dried onto the bracken. Many people have commented upon these primitive, simple methods of tradition; it may be seen, as Hamada pointed out, that they are not so simple after all. One pot done in this glaze was the original fish bottle (as I call it), which is in the Victoria and Albert Museum, but heavily mended . . .

Leach at work, 1932.

Dartington & Japan 1932–40

Bernard Leach

Extracts from
The Leach Pottery, 1920–1946,
published in connection with an
exhibition at the Berkeley Galleries,
London, 1946

In 1933 I went to teach, part-time at Dartington School, leaving David in charge for a month or two at a time. The Elmhirsts built a small pottery unit for me at Shinner's Bridge in which I developed the English slip-ware technique, using the chocolate-coloured Fremington clay from North Devon, which is the same as that used at Lake's Pottery, Truro, – the last of the traditional Cornish kilns. But I vitrified the body by taking the temperature to over 1000°C. and used an excellent black engobe or slip – often trailing white over black and dipping into transparent iron glaze so that the effect was yellow on shot black.

Life at Dartington was enriched with personal and artistic contacts and the intermingling of nationalities: Jooss Ballet, Tchehov drama, music under Hans Oppenheim, drawing, painting, sculpture and exhibitions of living art.

My closest friend was the American artist Mark Tobey with whom I travelled to the Far East in 1934. My old companions of art in Japan, particularly those associated with what had become a national craft movement, had invited me to revisit them and work in their several centres for a year. Leonard and Dorothy Elmhirst felt that such an invitation should not be refused and they not only financed me but also Mark.

This is no place in which to attempt to describe the happenings of that amazing year. As far as work was concerned it was the fullest in my life.

With Hamada in Mashiko, Tomimoto in Tokyo, Kawai in Kyoto, and Funaki in Matsue, and in three other potteries, the pots and drawings were done for eleven exhibitions. Besides that, with Yanagi as leader, we travelled 4,000 miles collecting examples of folk art, planning, lecturing, criticising. This work was rewarded by the promise of adequate funds for the building and maintenance of a beautiful National Museum of 'people's art'.

Some time after I got back I decided to leave David in charge once more. Laurie and I bought a car and caravan in which we lived for a time at Ditchling, then at Winchcombe near Michael Cardew, and finally at Dartington. There I began to write *A Potter's Book* for Richard de la Mare of Fabers. At the same time I resumed potting and a little teaching of adults besides making periodic visits to St Ives where David was making a number of technical improvements, including the successful installation of an oil-burner and air-blower in 1937. Then we gave up slipware in favour of stoneware because it suits the conditions of modern life better and offers a wider field of suggestion and experiment.

In 1940 my book was published. Despite the war it has sold well, both here and in the USA, and it has brought me friends and contacts with potters far and near. The first edition was curtailed by bombing, but a second has appeared and has twice been re-printed.

1940

Bernard Leach

Extracts from
A Potter's Book,
first published by Faber and Faber,
London, 1940

The range of plastic beauty achieved in primitive pottery, made chiefly by the hands of women without a wheel and with tools only of wood or stone, basketry, textiles, leaves of trees or stitched animal hides, is immense. The whole world seems to have contributed to it during thousands of prehistoric years: Minoan, archaic Greek, African, North and South American, pots of the Black Earth Region and neolithic China, pigmented but unglazed, often so fine that one might be tempted to surrender all claim for the supremacy of eleventh- and twelfth-century China, were it not for the fact that the general cultural and technical achievements of the Sung Chinese were so much greater.

Round the questions of accidentals and incidentals in pottery making revolve some of the chief difficulties we encounter in reaching a new idea of standard. After the symmetries and microscopic precision of mass production these two words seem such mouthfuls to swallow. But if T'ang or Sung pottery is accepted as the highest achievement in ceramics they will have to be swallowed. Eastern and Western thought alike regard man and his work as very inadequate and variable affairs, and an Oriental art lover eyes any very perfect piece of technique with the suspicion that it contains little depth of meaning. In all the greatest pottery of the world the natural limitations of both the material and the maker are accepted without question. In China the clays are often coarse and usually exposed, the glazes are thick, and crackled, and run, and occasionally skip, the brushwork is vigorous and calligraphic, not realistic and 'finished', the throwing and moulding are frank, and accidental kiln effects are frequent.

It is obvious that the standards of the world's best pottery, for example those of the T'ang and Sung periods in China and the best of the Ming, Korean celadons and Ri-cho, early Japanese tea-master's wares, early Persian, Syrian, Hispano-Moresque, German Bellarmines, some delft and English slipwares, cannot well be applied to industrial work, for such pottery was a completely unified human expression. It had not been mechanized. Yet there is no doubt that much can be learned by the industrial potter or designer from the wares especially of the Sung and early Ming dynasties. The Chinese potters' use of natural colours and textures in clays, the quality of their glazes (e.g. the Ying-ching and T'zu-chow families), the beauty and vitality of their well-balanced and proportioned forms, could be a constant source of inspiration to the designer for mass-production no less than to the craftsman.

'Accepting the Sung standard' is a very different thing from imitating particular Sung pieces. It means the use so far as possible of natural materials in the endeavour to obtain the best quality of body and glaze; in throwing and in a striving towards unity, spontaneity, and simplicity of form, and in general the subordination of all attempts at technical cleverness to straightforward, unselfconscious workmanship. A strict adherence to Chinese standards, however fine, cannot be advocated, for no matter what the source and power of a stimulus, what we make of it is the only thing that counts. We are not the Chinese of a thousand years ago, and the underlying racial and social and economic conditions which produced the Sung traditions in art will never be repeated; but that is no reason why we should not draw all the inspiration we can from the Sung potters.

In a broad way the difference between the old potters and the new is between unconsciousness within a single culture and individual consciousness of all cultures. And to this one can only add that until a life synthesis is reached by humanity the individual potter can only hope to deepen and widen his consciousness in anticipation and contribution towards that end.

Leach decorating with brushwork, 1948.

The Leach Pottery climbing kiln.

1940

Soetsu Yanagi/Bernard Leach

Extracts from
A Potter's Book,
first published by Faber and Faber,
London, 1940

'. . .Not beauty for beauty's own sake, but beauty answering all immediate needs of life – that is the essence of ceremonial tea . . .

One may ask, what then is the nature of the beauty which has been discovered by these tea-masters? . . . In the first place it is non-individualistic. . . . As in medieval Europe art meant adherence to tradition, so in the East all works of arts or crafts were governed equally by common principles. . . . Some of the most famous tea-bowls were originally the simplest of utensils in popular use in Korea or China; many of them were the rice bowls of Korean peasants. But the amazingly keen eye of the *Cha-no-yu* master has discovered in these odd, neglected pieces a unique beauty; for what most appeals to him are the things originally made for everyday use. In brief, *Cha-no-yu* may be defined as an aesthetics of actual living, in which utility is the first principle of beauty. And that is why such great significance has been given to certain articles necessary for everyday life . . . 'The next important aspect of the works of people's art is that they are simple and unassuming. Here the quality of extravagance that is always associated with expensive art objects is wholly absent, and any surplus of decorativeness is objectionable. Simplicity may be thought of as a characteristic of cheap things, but it must be remembered that it is a quality that harmonizes well with beauty. That which is truly beautiful is often simple and restrained . . . I am told that St Francis of Assisi advocated what he called 'Holy Poverty'. A thing possessed in some manner of the virtue of poverty has an indescribable beauty. Indeed, Beauty and Humility border upon each other. What is so appealing in the art of the people is this very quality, . . . beauty accompanied by the nobleness of poverty. The Japanese people have a special word *shibui* to express this ideal beauty. . . . It is impossible to translate it satisfactorily into one English term, 'austere', 'subdued', 'restrained', these words come nearest. Etymologically, *shibui* means 'astringent', and is used to describe profound, unassuming and quiet feeling. The mere fact that we have such an adjective would not call for second thought, but what does call for special note is the fact that this adjective is the final criterion for the highest form of beauty.'

Mr Yanagi seems to me in these arresting and moving sentences to have thrown down a challenge not only to his Japanese contemporaries but to us as well – a challenge to our over-accentuated individualism. For one may indeed look back with an acute sense of loss to those periods when the communal element, with its native religious psychological and aesthetic basis, was all-powerful as an ennobling and transmuting influence and source of life.

Bernard Leach

Author's dedication for
A Potter's Portfolio,
published by Lund Humphries,
London, 1951

THIS VOLUME IS DEDICATED
TO THE UNKNOWN POTTER

So doth the potter sitting at his work, and turning the wheel about with his feet...

He fashioneth the clay with his arm, and boweth down his strength before his feet; he applieth himself to lead it over; and he is diligent to make clean the furnace. All these trust to their hands: and everyone is wise in his work...

Without these cannot a city be inhabited...

They shall not be sought for in public counsel, nor sit high in the congregation...

But they will maintain the state of the world, and (all) their desire is in the work of their craft.

ECCLESIASTICUS 38

Every improvement in the standard of work men do is followed swiftly and inevitably by an improvement in the men who do it.

WILLIAM MORRIS

1951

Bernard Leach

Extract from
A Potter's Portfolio,
published by Lund Humphries,
London, 1951

Aesthetically a pot may be analysed for its abstract content or as a humanistic expression; subjectively or objectively; for its relationships of pure form or for its manner or hand-writing and suggestion of source of emotional content. It may be coolly intellectual, or warmly emotional, or any combination of such opposite tendencies. Whatever school it belongs to, however, the shape and pattern must, I believe, conform to inner principles of growth which can be felt even if they cannot be easily fathomed by intellectual analysis. Every movement hangs like frozen music in delicate but precise tension. Volumes, open spaces and outlines are parts of a living whole; they are thoughts, controlled forces in counterpoise of rhythm. A single intuitive pressure on the spinning wet clay and the whole pot comes to life; a false touch and the expression is lost. Of twenty similar pots on a board, all made to weight and measure in the same number of minutes, only one may have that life. A potter on his wheel is doing two things at the same time: he is making hollow wares to stand upon a level surface for the common usage of the home, and he is exploring space. His endeavour is determined in one respect by use, but in other ways by a never-ending search for perfection of form. Between the subtle opposition and interplay of centrifugal and gravitational force, between straight and curve (ultimately of sphere and cylinder, the hints of which can be seen between the foot and lip of every pot), are hidden all the potter's experience of beauty. Under his hands the clay responds to emotion and thought from a long past, to his own intuition of the lovely and the true, accurately recording the stages of his own inward development. The pot is the man: his virtues and his vices are shown therein – no disguise is possible.

Leach with Hamada and Yanagi watching
Maria Martinez unpacking a firing
in New Mexico, 1952.

1960

Bernard Leach

Extract from
A Potter in Japan,
published by Faber and Faber,
London, 1960

I would like to make a plea both as an English craftsman, and as an old participant in Japanese Crafts, for the workshop as the proper place for the transference of craft skills from one generation to another. With the decay of traditional right ways of making things, which are both useful and beautiful, developed out of centuries of communal experience, we have arrived at a stage where only a handful of artists or craftsmen in any industrialized country produce work of real and lasting value. The natural desire of these artist–craftsmen is to make, and teaching is a secondary issue. The fact is that with us there are not enough sound craftsmen to teach the teachers, with the result that a very high percentage of craft instructors are theorists with amateur skills.

Two problems are involved: first, craft teaching as a part of general education; secondly; the professional training of craftsmen. The more highly industrialized a country the greater the shortage of teachers for either purpose. What we need to rectify in the West is the spread through education of superficial and false ideas about crafts. No training whatever would be preferable to much that is going on.

Leach at Hamada's pottery,
Mashiko, Japan, 1971.

1975

Bernard Leach

Extracts from
The Potter's Challenge,
published by Souvenir Press, London,
and E. P. Dutton, New York, 1976

In making pots one of the great pleasures I have had is in using a good clay to pull a handle. Pulling is done by taking a slightly hardish lump of clay with a wet hand constantly dipped in water to keep it lubricated. Take that lump of clay and form it by the thumb pressing it inside and the hollow of your hand on the outside until it looks like you are milking the teat of a cow. You put pressure down the edge on one side, then you do it on the other side until it has the desired thickness and ribbing, so that the handle will be nice to use, nice to pour with. You get pleasure in the making, there is pleasure to you in using, pleasure to your friends, pleasure in the work. That is the kind of pleasure I have had, and I think perhaps the greatest. I am fairly good at making a handle and I have taught many potteries of Japan how to make a handle of the pulled kind, which they never had in their past. The pleasure comes in keeping the same width to hold comfortably when pouring. How the jug balances best, not only empty but full of liquid, is determined by the handle and its line, which should swing through to the spout or lip. The handle should be strong in attachment so that is carries the weight. Its base should come off the side like the branch of a beech tree. I like to see where the angle is, not just the slick S-curve. Every curve has a bone in it, just as every arm has a bone in it, and to make it a sweet line of single or double curve is not giving enough appreciation of construction and materials. Usually it is well to have an inch or more coming straight off an extra ridge along the top of the jug. That is the natural jumping off place. It should be half the width of the average hand for a full-size jug, and it should stay far enough away from the pitcher so that your knuckles won't be burned.

. . . .

In the pots of the world that we consider the best – Korean of the Yi dynasty and Chinese Sung – this quality of life comes out of what was essentially *repeat work*. These rice and soup bowls that we admire were made by the thousands. In the Leach Pottery, where we usually have several student potters, I have always said that by making a lot of similar pots by hand (of a shape you like), an expansion of the true spirit at the expense of the lesser ego is bound to take place. There are two parts to each of us: the surface man who is concerned with pose and position, who thinks what he has been taught to think; and the real man who responds to nature and seeks life in his work.

How then does repeat work fall into the scheme of the young potter today? They are so keen on one-of-a-kind, they want so much to be artists that the acceptance of work for life's sake has been lost.

In Japan, beauty has always been related to humility, and the best potters are some of the most humble who do not need to display themselves by a shelf of pots all of contrived differences in shape and colour. Repeat work is like making good bread. That is what it is, and although one is doing repeat work it is not really deadly repetition; nothing is ever quite the same; never, cannot be. That is where the pleasure lies.

1975

Bernard Leach

Extracts from
The Potter's Challenge,
published by Souvenir Press, London,
and E. P. Dutton, New York, 1976

Because of the very smoothness of perfection we yearn for imperfection. Imperfection – irregularity – is a necessity. We are ourselves imperfect: our noses are crooked, one eye is nearer the bridge of the nose than the other, and so on right through the whole body. Trees are asymmetrical and irregular; the sand and rocks on a beach are also. In all of nature there is this asymmetry; not too much, but a degree of it, and it provides the sense of vitality of life.

It is a big word, work, and it covers our principal occupation on this globe. Of the world's pots I would choose the Korean above all. The last thing in the world those people would think is that they were artists or craftsmen. They were people doing work as well as they knew how and getting as much satisfaction as a man could. In their pots this is revealed through an innocence, a nonchalance, a closeness to nature which shows itself, and not the man.

This Clay

Bernard Leach

Published in the Sunday Mainichi, and read by the author in the New Wing, Otago Museum, 9 February 1962
From *Drawings, Verse and Belief*, published by Jupiter Books, London, 1977

This earth upon which we stand: of which we are made: of which we
    make pots;
This volcanic rock, eroded, exploded – ashes to ashes.
Earth quivers in Japan, shaken by internal fires,
It grows bamboo shoots, a foot a day –
June sends them up roof high.
In Cornwall we live on ancient granite rock
Standing against Atlantic surges, feet firm upon a ground that grows no
    trees whilst all winds blow.
Northern clouds roll over a rolling sea and wrap our granite hills in mist,
Grass grows green throughout the year,
And spring comes stepping tenderly with flowers along our rocky paths.
When I go back memories will wake with me at dawn of waters running
    fast from mountains to the sea.
I shall see the maple burn upon the slopes, and the cherry fall, in dreams.
My friends, no doubt, will talk of me but I shall not go out at night and
    feast with them on beans and fish, on buckwheat and on flesh.
The wonder of the rice fields on all flat land from coast to coast:
Women in spotted indigo bending over the earth, tending it with love as
    if it were a child:
Anxious old farmers peering at their crops early in the morning, or as
    night falls.
Blue smoke rising to the mists which wreath among the pine clad hills:
Twinkle of silver bird-scares hung across the ripening grain: voices of
    semi (cicadae) and of frogs – frogs in the mud.

Clay spinning on a potter's wheel,
Clay spinning on wheels all over Japan:
Clay in man, clay on the wheel spinning like the earth and the stars, man
    spinning the clay into stars.
Life spinning the man – LIFE.

Tributes

Leach at Yanagi's house in Japan,
1954.

1920

Soetsu Yanagi

Extract from
An English Artist in Japan,
privately printed in Tokyo, 1920

I believe his pottery is going to hold a distinguished position in the artistic world of today ... When Leach has more experience I am quite sure he will become known as the creator of some eternal masterpieces. He is fertile in design, possesses fine discrimination for form and quality, and an intuitive sense of beauty. He has a depth of feeling that goes beyond mere technique, the character of an artist who will be satisfied with nothing short of work that will live.

In the aim that he set himself in his artistic work from this year forward, 'that it should be practically useful without losing its beauty', he reveals his first aim once more.

I believe in his character, and I believe in his art ... I believe in his future. He is a man who came to the East with a definite purpose and is leaving with it fulfilled.

Many people fall in love with Japan and come to visit us, but there are few cases of people who are able to live here in the spirit of Japan ... He is the only one who has really lived as one of the most spiritually hungry young men of Japan.

1960

Michael Cardew

Extracts from
Bernard Leach – Recollections,
published in a special issue on the artist in
the New Zealand Potter,
Wellington, 1960

One hates to use ready-made phrases; but in the early nineteen twenties he really was a voice crying in the wilderness, and his work was, to an extent distressing to him and discreditable to the British public, despised and rejected. That public was not yet ready for such deliberately 'unshowy' work.

Leach's potting life has been that of a great pioneer, and his influence has perhaps been greatest on those who from conviction or necessity or temperament (or all three) have the pioneer's approach to pottery. His principles, sometimes explicit and sometimes implied, may be said to have been these: Pottery is a fundamental craft and should be pursued in a fundamental way. Beware of all 'short cuts'. Begin at the beginning. The simplest materials and the simplest methods are often the best. The most primitive work is often the most refined. Potters must be artists, but they should make things that are useful as well as decorative, otherwise they are in danger of losing the common touch. Teapots, cups, dishes, casseroles, are just as interesting as pots for flowers, for 'Eternity is in love with the productions of Time'.

1966

Shoji Hamada

Extract from
Bernard Leach, The Man and His Works,
published by Asahi Shimbun, Tokyo,
1966

Leach began his study of *Raku* ware in Tokyo under Ogata Kenzan VI over fifty years ago. He then embarked on the study of stoneware and later returned to England and taught the Eastern methods of making pottery. In all these endeavours Leach had his feet firmly planted in the East and the West. Never losing the fresh outlook of the beginner, he cultivated his art without haste. He has applied himself to this art for over half a century and still retains the wonderful qualities of the amateur. This is something that rarely occurs. Leach came by these qualities through a rigorous self-discipline and desisted from undertaking what did not suit his temperament and sought no greater technical skill than he found necessary.

In a profession in which one can easily get lost in the fascinations of technical skill such as in glazes, it is easy to fall into the temptation without realizing it and end up being a pseudo-professional for whom technical skill is all that matters. I am grateful to Leach for the noble spirit that enabled him to retain the fresh outlook of the beginner all these years, for he set an example and has helped me manage to travel the road of my profession without straying.

1972

Shoji Hamada

Extract from his foreword to
The Unknown Craftsman,
published by Kodansha, Tokyo, 1972

The feeling in his pots comes from a high inspiration that defeats both weakened traditions and the violence of modern motivation I have mentioned. He draws his strength from the soil of his own nature and his life experience. This is spring water. I feel the difference between this inspiration and that of others very strongly. His stance between East and West is a true balance, not a measured middle.

Bernard Leach: Chronology

1887   5th January, born in Hong Kong.
        His mother dies and grandparents take him to Japan.

1890   Returns to Hong Kong when father remarries.

1894   Moves to Singapore when his father is appointed a
        British Colonial Judge.

1897   To school in England at Beaumont Jesuit College, near
        Windsor.

1903   Slade School of Art, studies drawing under Henry
        Tonks.

1904   November, father dies.

1905   Studies in Manchester for entry to Hong Kong and
        Shanghai Bank.

1908   London School of Art, studies etching under Frank
        Brangwyn.

1909   To Japan. Builds house in Tokyo.
        Marries cousin Muriel Hoyle.
        Exhibits his etchings and proposes to teach this
        technique.

1910   Friendship with Kenkichi Tomimoto.

1911   *Yaki raku* tea party, meets members of Shirakaba Society.
        Friendship with Soetsu Yanagi.
        Exhibits work with Tomimoto and others and
        subsequently with Shirakaba Society.
        Meets potter Ogata Kenzan.
        Son David born.

1913   Son Michael born.
        Kenzan builds kiln in Leach's workshop.

1914   *A Review 1909–1914*, his first publication, and first one-
        man show in Tokyo.

1915   Family moves to Peking.
        Daughter Eleanor born.

1916   Yanagi visits Leach in Peking.
        Family returns to Japan and Leach rebuilds Kenzan's kiln
        on Yanagi's property.

1918   Visits Korea with Yanagi.

1919   Meets Shoji Hamada.
        Workshop burns down.
        Exhibition in Tokyo.

1920   Final exhibition in Japan.
        Leaves for England with family and Hamada.
        Twin daughters, Betty and Jessamine born in Cardiff.
        With Hamada establishes pottery at St Ives, Cornwall,
        building first oriental climbing kiln in Europe.

1921   Exhibition: Artificers' Guild, London.

1922   First English one-man exhibition: Cotswold Gallery,
        London.
        T. Matsubayashi joins St Ives, designs and rebuilds kiln.

1923   Michael Cardew comes to St Ives as Leach's first student.
        Hamada returns to Japan.
        Exhibitions: Paterson's Gallery and Three Shields
        Gallery, both in London, and in Japan.

1924   Katherine Pleydell-Bouverie joins St Ives Pottery.
        Exhibitions: Japan.
        Matsubayashi returns to Japan.

1925   Norah Braden joins St Ives Pottery.
        Exhibitions: Japan.

1927   Exhibition: Three Shields Gallery, London.

1928   *A Potter's Outlook* published.
        Exhibition: Beaux Arts Gallery, London.

1929   Yanagi and Hamada visit St Ives Pottery.

1930   Son David joins pottery.

1931   Exhibition: (with Tomimoto) Beaux Arts Gallery,
        London.

1932   Begins teaching at Dartington Hall, Devon.
        Meets painter Mark Tobey.
        Becomes interested in the Baha'i Faith.
        Exhibition: The Little Gallery, London.

1933   Exhibition: (with Tomimoto) Beaux Arts Gallery,
        London.

1934   Invited to Japan by National Craft Society.
        Travels in Japan with Yanagi and Hamada in search of
        country crafts. Works at 7 potteries (including
        Hamada's, Tomimoto's, and Kawai's).
        Exhibitions: Matsuzakaya and Takashimaya. Makes
        slipware at Matsue.

1935   Visits Korea, returns to England.

1936   Resumes teaching at Dartington Hall in newly built
        pottery.
        Exhibition: The Little Gallery, London.

1937   End of slipware production at St Ives.
        Change from wood to oil firing.

1938   William Marshall joins St Ives Pottery.

1940   *A Potter's Book* published.
        Declares his belief in the Baha'i Faith.

1944   Marries Laurie Cookes.

1946   *The Leach Pottery 1920–1946* published in association with
        exhibition at the Berkeley Galleries, London 1946.

1949   Exhibitions: Gothenburg, Sweden; Oslo, Norway;
        Copenhagen, Denmark.
        Guest of Danish Arts and Crafts Society.

1950   Tours USA for four months.
        Travelling exhibition organised by ICA, Washington.

1951   *A Potter's Portfolio* published.

1952   Exhibition: (with Hamada) Beaux Arts Gallery,
        London.
        International Crafts Conference, at Dartington Hall.
        Far East represented by Yanagi and Hamada, who join
        Leach on American tour reporting conference and
        Yanagi's aesthetic.

1953   Trio continue tour in Japan.
        Leach lectures, works, exhibits.

1954   Returns to England.

1955   Sons David and Michael leave St Ives to establish their
        own potteries.

1956   Marries Janet Darnell, who gradually takes over
        management of St Ives Pottery.

1957   Exhibition: Liberty & Co., London.

1958   Exhibitions: Primavera, London, and travelling
        exhibitions in USA.

1960   *A Potter in Japan* published.
        A Potter's World BBC film of St Ives Pottery.

1961   Hon.D.Litt. Exeter.
        Yanagi dies.
        'Fifty Years a Potter', retrospective exhibition, Arts
        Council Gallery, London.
        Visits Japan in connection with exhibition of medieval
        English pottery and retrospective exhibition of own
        work in Osaka.
        Visits Australia, New Zealand, USA.

1962   Returns to England.
        Made Commander of the British Empire (CBE).
        Exhibitions: Primavera, London, and (with Hamada)
        Louvre, Paris.

1963   Tomimoto dies.

1964   Attends Japanese Folk Crafts meeting in Okinawa.
        Exhibitions: Tokyo, and Primavera, London.

1966 Exhibitions: Primavera, London; and (with Hamada and Francine del Pierre) Museo de Bellas Artes, Caracas, Venezuela, and National Museum, Popayan, Colombia, then visits Japan for retrospective exhibition in Tokyo. Receives Order of the Sacred Treasure, second class. *Kenzan and his Tradition* published.

1967 *A Potter's Work* published.
Exhibitions: Crane Kalman Gallery, London; (with Hamada and Kawai) at Osaka, Japan; and (with Hamada and Francine del Pierre) at Museum für Kunst und Gewerbe, Hamburg.

1968 Exhibition: (with Lucie Rie and Janet Leach) at Primavera, London.

1969 Visits Japan, exhibition in Okinawa.

1970 World Crafts Council honour.

1971 Exhibitions: Marjorie Parr Gallery, London; and retrospective show at Tenmaya, Okayama.

1972 Sight failing, stops potting.
The Unknown Craftsman published.

1973 Visits Japan for exhibition at Tenmaya, Okayama. On return to England made Companion of Honour (CH).
Drawings, Verse and Belief published.

1974 Japanese Foundation Cultural Award. NHK Television film.

1975 *Hamada: Potter* published.

1976 *A Potter's Challenge* published.

1977 'The Art of Bernard Leach', major retrospective exhibition at the Victoria & Albert Museum, London.

1978 Hamada dies.
Beyond East and West published.

1

2

3

4

5

6

1

12

13

26

27

31

33

TILE PICTURE
LEACH

34

35

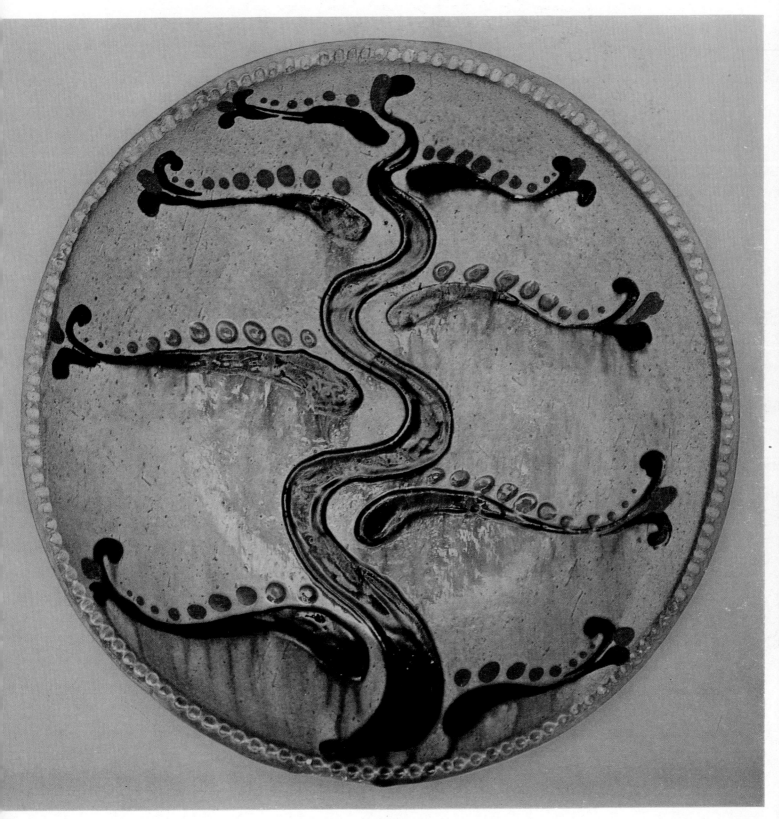

45

52

53

54

55

67

68

69

70

73

74

77

104

105

115

116

117

Drawings and etchings

124

125

Karuizawa raging Winds.   *BL* 1912

126

Bamboos + a Japanese hut. 1914   *BL*

127

128

129

30

132

133

134

135

136

137

138

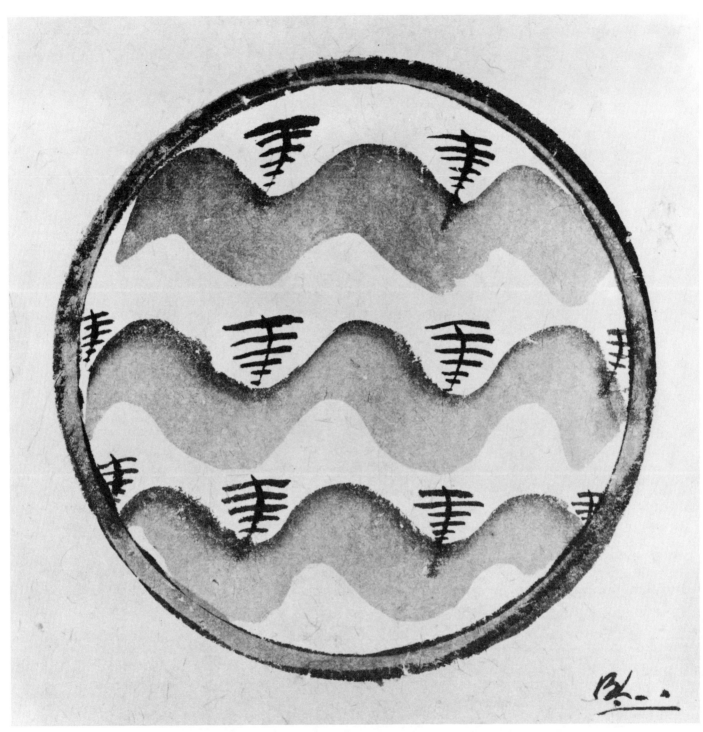

140

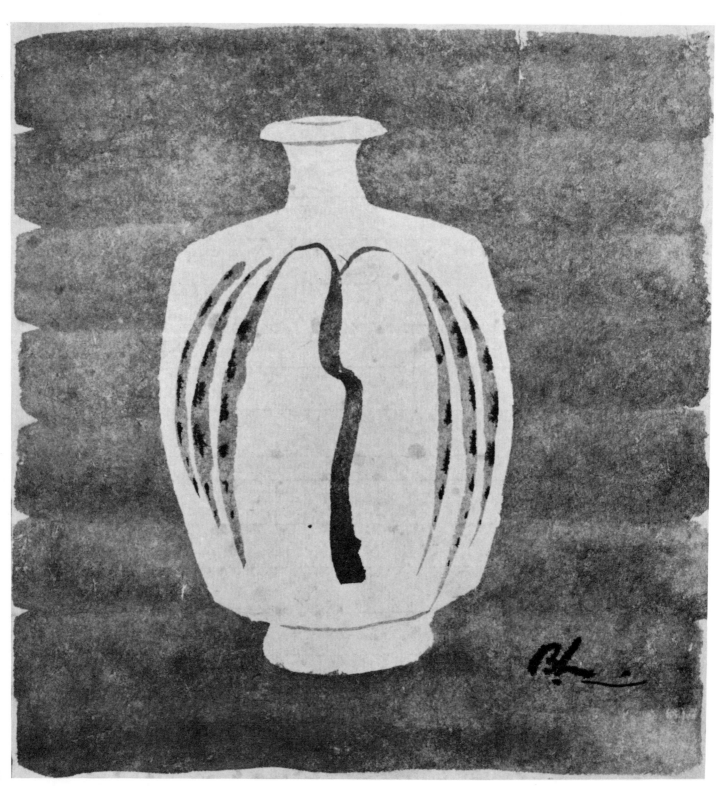

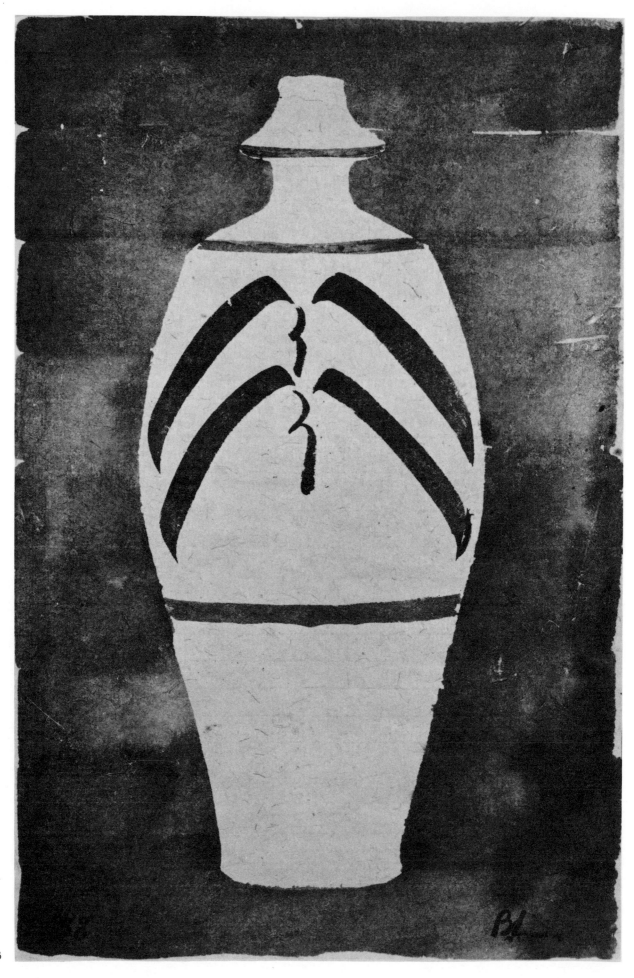

Descriptions of the illustrations

Pots

subjects reproduced in colour are marked *

1
Vase, porcelain, decorated with oriental scenes in blue on a white ground. Made in Tokyo, 1912.
Height 16cm./6¼in. Mark: 'B.H.L., painted in Japan after a Chinese piece, 1912,' painted.
Collection: David Leach

2
Small tea bowl, stoneware, decorated in white slip on a speckled grey ground. Made at Abiko, 1917.
Diameter 7.4cm./2⅞in.
Collection: Crafts Study Centre, Bath

3
Lidded pot, porcelain, decorated with oriental scenes in blue on a white ground. Made at Kenzan's pottery in Tokyo, 1912–13.
Diameter 10cm./4in. Mark: B.H.L., painted.
Collection: the artist

4*
Model of the workshop and kiln at Abiko, raku, incised decoration and coloured with red and blue slip on a cream ground. Made at Abiko, 1917.
Length 17.5cm./6⅞in. Mark: BL, impressed in circular seal.
Collection: Crafts Study Centre, Bath

5*
Another view of 3

6*
Tea mug (Unomi), stoneware, with incised decoration through a white slip showing Leach's workshop and kiln at Abiko, and commemorating its first successful firing.
Height 9cm./3½in. Mark: '1919 ABIKO KINEN BL,' incised with the decoration.
Collection: Crafts Study Centre, Bath

7
Another view of 6

8
Another view of 6

9
Part of coffee set: coffee pot, sugar bowl, and five cups and saucers, stoneware, with celadon glaze. Made in Tokyo, 1919.
Greatest height 11cm./4¼in. Mark: BL, impressed in circular seal.
Collection: Mrs Dicon Nance

10
Vase, stoneware, decorated with matt light brown over a shiny, dark brown tenmoku glaze. Made at St Ives, 1921.
Height 14cm./5½in. Mark: BL SI, impressed in circular seals.

Collection: Victoria & Albert Museum, London

11
Jug, earthenware, yellow galena glaze on white slip, with sgraffito decoration of a snowdrop and a quotation from William Blake: 'A little flower is the labour of ages'. Made at St Ives, 1921–2.
Height 12.7cm./5in. Mark: WB BL, incised with the decoration; SI, impressed in circular seal.
Collection: Crafts Study Centre, Bath

12
Another view of 11

13*
Vase, raku, the sides decorated with incised curved lines with blue and brown colouring on a cream ground. Made in Tokyo, 1913.
Height 14cm./5½in. Mark: BL, incised.
Collection: the artist

14*
Dish, raku, decorated in brown and blue slip on a cream ground, with a skylark in the centre and lines by William Blake on the rim. Made at Abiko, 1917.
Diameter 20.5cm./8in.. Mark: B.H.L. 1917, in trailed slip.
Collection: the artist

15
Bowl with lip, raku, circular on a raised foot. It has a cream glaze; the top rim is decorated with a band of cream and red scrolls on a blue ground. Made at St Ives, about 1923.
Diameter 21.5cm./8½in. Mark: BL SI, impressed in circular seals.
Collection: Mr Bruce and Mrs Monica Wightman

16
Vase, earthenware, with a flared top and yellow galena glaze on white slip; with sgraffito decoration of a griffon and the date 1923. Made at St Ives, 1923.
Height 15.2cm./6in. Mark: BL SI, impressed in circular seals.
Collection: Victoria & Albert Museum, London

17
Biscuit barrel, earthenware, with inset lid and yellow galena glaze on white cut slip; decorated with birds and clouds. Made at St Ives, 1923–4.
Diameter 15cm./5⅞in. Mark: BL SI, impressed in circular seals.
Collection: Victoria & Albert Museum, London

18
Incense burner, stoneware, with an undulating pierced top surmounted by a bird. Celadon glaze. Made at St Ives, about 1923–4.
Height 16cm./6¼in. Mark: BL SI, impressed in circular seals.
Collection: Stoke-on-Trent Museum and Art Gallery

19*
Vase, earthenware, yellow galena glaze on white cut slip; decorated with a bird and flowers. Made at St Ives, 1922–3.
Height 17cm./6¾in. Mark: BL SI, impressed in circular seals.
Collection: Mr Bruce and Mrs Monica Wightman

20*
Dish, lead-glazed earthenware, a shallow bowl decorated with a tree of life pattern at the centre and a border of fish, in brown slip on a yellow ground. Made at St Ives, 1923. Diameter 42.3cm./16¾in.
Mark: BL 1923, in coloured slip.
Collection: Victoria & Albert Museum, London

21
Lidded jar, stoneware. A small, square-sided, moulded jar with a domed lid; with a purplish-black glaze and a wax-resist decoration. Made at St Ives, 1924.
Height 15.6cm./6⅛in. Mark: BL SI, impressed.
Collection: Miss Muriel Rose

22
Bowl, high-fired slipware with a decoration of curved lines in dark brown against a mottled green ground. Made at St Ives, 1924–5.
Diameter 25cm./9⅞in. Mark: SI, impressed in circular seal.
Collection: Mr Bruce and Mrs Monica Wightman

23
Another view of 22

24
Vase, stoneware; cut sides and an impressed pattern with four lugs at the shoulder; mottled green and blue glaze. Made at St Ives, about 1925–6.
Height 18.5cm./7¼in. Mark: BL SI, impressed in circular seals.
Collection: Kingston upon Thames Museum and Art Gallery

25*
Vase, earthenware, with yellow galena glaze on white slip; with sgraffito decoration of tree forms on a textured ground. Made at St Ives, about 1923.
Height 18.5cm./7¼in. Mark: BL, incised; SI, impressed in circular seal.
Collection: National Museum of Wales, Cardiff

26*
Vase, stoneware, with mottled green and brown glaze and added brown decoration. Made at St Ives, 1923–4.
Diameter 19cm./7½in. Mark: BL SI, impressed in circular seals.
Collection: Victoria & Albert Museum, London

27
Vase, stoneware, with a mottled grey and buff chün type glaze. Made at St Ives, about 1925.

Height 16cm./6¼in. Mark: BL, impressed in circular seal.
Collection: University College of Wales, Aberystwyth

28
Bowl, stoneware, with cut sides and a mottled brown and buff matt glaze, resulting from salt action on a celadon glaze. Made at St Ives, 1925–6.
Diameter 13.5cm./5¼in. Mark: BL SI, impressed in circular seals.
Collection: Victoria & Albert Museum, London

29
Bowl, stoneware, with flared rim and raised foot; with a rust and dark brown kaki to tenmoku glaze. Made at St Ives, 1924–5.
Diameter 27cm./10⅝in. Mark: BL, in rectangular seal; SI in circular seal; impressed.
Collection: City Art Gallery, Manchester

30
Bowl, stoneware, decorated with buff rim and floral spots on a rust red ground. Made at St Ives, 1925–6.
Diameter 12.7cm./5in. Mark: BL, in rectangular seal; SI in circular seal; impressed.
Collection: Victoria & Albert Museum, London

31*
Vase, stoneware, decorated with floral spots and a wavy pattern at top and bottom in dark slip under a celadon glaze. Made at St Ives, about 1925.
Height 16.5cm./6½in. Mark: BL SI, impressed in circular seals.
Collection: Victoria & Albert Museum, London

32*
Vase, stoneware, circular with fluted sides; speckled light and dark brown glaze. Made at St Ives, 1925–6.
Height 24.5cm./9⅝in. Mark: BL SI, impressed in circular seals.
Collection: Dartington Hall Trust

33
Tile from the panel described below, 34, showing a three-chambered, climbing kiln.

34
Panel of tiles, stoneware. Forty-nine small square tiles; twenty-five of them decorated with pictorial images in brown and blue on a cream ground, alternating with plain mottled buff tiles, with a border of small rectangular brown tiles. The whole set in a wooden frame. About 1928.
Width 98.8cm./38⅞in. (frame). Mark: BL SI, signed on most of the pictorial tiles as part of decoration.
Collection: York City Art Gallery

35
Panel of tiles, stoneware. Nine square tiles

decorated with animal and landscape subjects in brown and blue on a mottled buff ground; set in a wooden frame. Made at St Ives, about 1928.
Width 94cm./37in. (frame). Mark: BL SI, signed on some tiles as part of decoration.
Collection: Mr Bruce and Mrs Monica Wightman

36
Panel of tiles, stoneware. Nine square tiles decorated with an overall picture of a well-head in a mountainous landscape, in shades of brown on a mottled cream ground; set in a wooden frame. Made at St Ives, about 1928.
Width 83.5cm./32⅞in. (frame). Mark: BL, on bottom right-hand tile; SI on bottom left-hand tile; painted as part of decoration.
Collection: York City Art Gallery

37
Large dish, earthenware, decorated with two birds in the centre and a pattern trailed criss-cross on the rim; in orange and brown slip on a yellow ground. Made at St Ives, 1926.
Diameter 49cm./19¼in. Mark: BL 1926, in coloured slip.
Collection: Merseyside County Museums, Liverpool

38*
Large dish, earthenware, decorated with a griffon in the centre and a pattern of crossed lines on the rim; in brown slips on a yellow ground. Made at St Ives, 1929.
Diameter 45.7cm./18in. Mark: BL 1929, in coloured slip.
Collection: Mr and Mrs George Wingfield Digby

39*
Large dish, earthenware, decorated with an oriental landscape, 'The Mountains', in the centre; in brown slips on a yellow ground. Made at St Ives, 1929.
Diameter 45cm./17¾in. Mark: BL 1929, in coloured slip.
Collection: Royal Institution of Cornwall, Truro

40
Vase, stoneware, with an oriental landscape pattern painted in blue on a grey celadon ground. Made at St Ives, about 1926.
Height 20cm./7⅞in. Mark: BL, in rectangular seal; SI, in circular seal; impressed. BL, painted in blue.
Collection: Mr Richard Dennis

41
Vase, porcelain, decorated with sea serpents in blue on a pale blue ground. Made at St Ives, about 1927.
Diameter 15.2cm./6in. Mark: BL SI, impressed in circular seals.
Collection: Mr Peter Rainsford

42
Vase, stoneware, with light brown

patterning on dark brown; iron decorated tenmoku. Made at St Ives, about 1928.
Diameter 17.5cm./6⅞in. Mark: BL, in rectangular seal; SI, in circular seal; impressed.
Collection: Mr Ian Bennett

43
Jug, earthenware, decorated with the Cornish arms and motto, fifteen balls and 'ONE & ALL'; cut through light slip under a yellow glaze. Made at St Ives, 1929.
Height 26.5cm./10½in. Mark: BL, in rectangular seal; SI, in circular seal; impressed.
Collection: City Art Gallery, Manchester

44*
Dish, earthenware, decorated with a tree; in brown slips on a yellow ground. Made at St Ives, about 1930.
Diameter 31.2cm./12¼in. Mark: SI, impressed in circular seal.
Collection: Mrs Bertha Bundy

45*
Dish, earthenware, decorated with a tree; in light combed slip on a dark brown ground. Made at St Ives, about 1930.
Diameter 30cm./11⅞in. Mark: BL SI, impressed in circular seals.
Collection: Victoria & Albert Museum, London

46
Large dish, earthenware, decorated with an oriental landscape, 'The Mountains', in the centre; in brown slips on a yellow ground. Made at St Ives, about 1930.
Diameter 51.5cm./20¼in. Mark: BL, in brown slip.
Collection: Dartington Hall Trust

47
Bowl, stoneware, decorated with a pattern of curved lines, cut and sgraffito under a celadon glaze. Made at St Ives, about 1930.
Diameter 19cm./7½in. Mark: BL, in rectangular seal; SI, in circular seal; impressed.
Collection: Dartington Hall Trust

48
Bowl, stoneware, decorated with a fish in sgraffito under a celadon glaze. Made at St Ives, about 1930.
Diameter 18.2cm./7⅛in. Mark: BL, in rectangular seal; SI, in circular seal: impressed.
Collection: City Museum and Art Gallery, Bristol

49
Vase, stoneware, with a speckled matt white glaze, decorated with four rows of leaping fish in brown. Made at St Ives, about 1931.
Height 34cm./13⅜in. Mark: BL, in rectangular seal; SI, in circular seal; impressed.
Collection: Victoria & Albert Museum, London

50★
Vase, lead-glazed earthenware, with three handles, decorated with three animals and the words 'GOD WITH US'; sgraffito on light slip with added dark brown colouring. Made at St Ives, about 1930.
Height 26cm./10¼in. Mark: BL, in rectangular seal; SI, in circular seal; impressed.
Collection: Mr Richard Dennis
51★
Vase, stoneware, the top two-thirds decorated with flower forms and dashes in brown on a light green ground. Made at St Ives, about 1930.
Height 20cm./7⅞in. Mark: BL, in rectangular seal; SI, in circular seal; impressed.
Collection: Mr Ian Bennett
52
Small tray, porcellaneous stoneware, decorated with a plant form in blue and yellow on a white ground. Made at St Ives, 1930–31.
Width 16.5cm./6½in. Mark: BL, incised and painted with the decoration; SI, impressed in circular seal.
Collection: Victoria & Albert Museum, London
53 (top left)
Lidded box, porcelain, decorated with oriental scenes in blue on a grey ground. Made at St Ives, about 1931.
Length 6.5cm./2½in. Mark: BL SI, incised.
Collection: Mr Colin Page
(top right)
Lidded box, moulded porcelain, decorated on the lid with two swallows in blue on a pale blue ground. Made in Kyoto, about 1934.
Length 12.7cm./5in. Mark: BL, in block letters; Kawai pottery mark; impressed in rectangular seals.
Collection: the artist
(bottom right)
Lidded box, porcelain, with a frog painted on the lid, in blue on a streaked grey ground. Made at St Ives, about 1942.
Width 6cm./2⅜in. Mark: BL, in rectangular seal; SI, in circular seal; impressed.
Collection: Miss Helen Pincombe.
(bottom centre)
Frog, stoneware, in light and dark brown, set on a square tile base. Made at St Ives, about 1926–7.
Width 5cm./2in. Mark: SI, impressed in circular seal.
Collection: Cecilia Lady Sempill
(bottom left)
Lidded box, porcelain, circular with a domed lid, decorated with bands of blue, buff and red. Made at St Ives, about 1958–60.
Diameter 7cm./2¾in. Mark: BL, block letters in rectangular seal; SI, in circular seal; impressed.
Private collection
54
Lidded pot, earthenware, slipware, decorated with two rows of dark brown spots on a yellow ground. Made at Dartington, about 1933.
Height 7.8cm./3⅛in. Mark: BL, impressed in rectangular seal.
Collection: the artist
55
Vase, stoneware, globular with four slightly flattened sides, each decorated with an incised spiral; with a speckled brown glaze. Made at St Ives, 1931.
Height 11.7cm./4⅞in. Mark: SI, in circular seal; impressed twice.
Collection: Southampton Art Gallery, Milner-White Collection
56
Vase, stoneware, with a white matt glaze, decorated with a leaping salmon and horizontal bands in dark brown. Made at St Ives, about 1931.
Height 32.5cm./12¾in. Mark: BL, in rectangular seal; SI, in circular seal; impressed. BL, painted with the decoration.
Collection: York City Art Gallery
57
Horse and rider, earthenware, with a mottled orange and yellow colouring. Intended to be set on a house roof ridge tile. Made at St Ives, 1931.
Length 41cm./16⅛in.
Collection: Miss Margaret Reed
58
Vase, stoneware, decorated with fish and plant forms on horizontal bands of light and dark grey. Made at St Ives, 1931.
Height 26cm./10¼in. Mark: BL, in rectangular seal; SI, in circular seal; impressed.
Collection: Victoria & Albert Museum, London
59
Vase, stoneware, decorated with an incised pattern of grey scrolls on a mottled buff ground. Made at St Ives, 1932.
Height 19.5cm./7⅝in. Mark: BL, in rectangular seal; SI, in circular seal; impressed.
Collection: Dartington Hall Trust
60
Vase, stoneware, with vertical grooves in the side; decorated with light wavy lines on a buff ground. Made at St Ives, 1933.
Height 24.5cm./9⅝in. Mark: BL, in rectangular seal; SI, in circular seal; impressed.
Collection: Southampton Art Gallery, Milner-White Collection
61
Jug, earthenware, undecorated black slipware. Made at Dartington, 1935.
Height 20cm./7⅞in. Mark: BL, impressed in rectangular seal.
Collection: the artist
62
Part of coffee set: jug, cream jug, sugar bowl and one of three cups and saucers, earthenware. Dark brown slipware decorated with a row of yellow spots. Made at Dartington, 1933.
Greatest height 14.3cm./5⅝in. Mark: BL, impressed in rectangular seal on most pieces.
Collection: Crafts Study Centre, Bath
63
Dish, earthenware, decorated with yellow, diagonal streaks against a rust coloured ground in combed slip. Made at St Ives, about 1934.
Length 40.6cm./16in. Mark: SI, impressed in square seal.
Collection: the artist
64
Vase, earthenware, cylindrical drug-jar form; dark brown slipware decorated with orange dots and waves. Made at Dartington, 1933.
Height 15.5cm./6⅛in. Mark: BL, impressed in rectangular seal.
Collection: Crafts Study Centre, Bath
65
Vase, stoneware, decorated with sgraffito lines under a mottled dark blue glaze. Made at St Ives, 1937–8.
Height 20cm./7⅞in. Mark: BL, in rectangular seal; SI, in circular seal; impressed.
Collection: Mrs Edward Malins
66
Biscuit barrel, stoneware, with a slightly domed lid; decorated with bands of light blue with brown wavy lines. Made at St Ives, 1943.
Height 28cm./11in. Mark: BL SI, impressed block letters in rectangular seals.
Collection: Cecilia Lady Sempill
67
Bowl, porcellaneous stoneware, decorated in the centre with the figure of a Korean washerwoman in pale cream colour on a light brown ground. Made at St Ives, about 1936.
Diameter 34cm./13⅜in. Mark: BL SI, lightly incised and painted.
Collection: Victoria & Albert Museum, London
68
Another view of 67
69
Tile, stoneware, with painted decoration of a Cornish tin mine. Made at St Ives, 1948.
Width 22cm./8⅝in. Mark: BL, '48, painted; SI, in circular seal; impressed.
Collection: Mr Henry Rothschild

70
Tile, stoneware, with a mottled buff glaze decorated with a John Dory fish in brown. Made at St Ives, about 1945.
Width 22.5cm./$8\frac{7}{8}$in. Mark: BL SI, painted as part of the decoration.
Collection: Stoke-on-Trent Museum and Art Gallery

71
Vase, stoneware, with a grey surface speckled with brown. Made at St Ives, 1945–50.
Height 38.5cm./$15\frac{1}{8}$in. Mark: BL, block letters in rectangular seal; SI, in circular seal; impressed.
Collection: Mrs Gwendolen Mullins

72
Jug, stoneware, decorated on the front with an embossed cross motif, and covered with a speckled grey glaze. Made at St Ives, 1945–6.
Height 38cm./15in. Mark: BL SI, impressed block letters in rectangular seals.
Collection: The British Council

73
Vase, stoneware, decorated with rectangular scenes of animals and mountains alternating with vertical stripes, in brown on a buff ground. Made at St Ives, about 1950.
Height 27cm./$10\frac{5}{8}$in. Mark: BL, block letters in rectangular seal; SI, in circular seal; impressed.
Collection: Leicestershire Museum and Art Gallery, Leicester

74
Vase, stoneware, covered with a thick red-brown glaze, decorated with two bands of incised leaf pattern. Made at St Ives, about 1945–6.
Height 23cm./9in. Mark: BL SI, impressed block letters in rectangular seals.
Private collection

75
Teapot, stoneware with cane handle, decorated around the top with blue dashes and dark spots on a speckled buff ground. Made at St Ives, 1951.
Height 22cm./$8\frac{5}{8}$in. Mark: SI, impressed in rectangular seal.
Collection: Mr and Mrs George Wingfield Digby

76*
Vase, stoneware, with a speckled matt white glaze, decorated with two sprays of flowers. Made at St Ives, about 1931.
Height 31cm./$12\frac{1}{4}$in. Mark: BL, in rectangular seal, SI, in circular seal; impressed.
Collection: City Art Gallery, Manchester

77*
Large dish, earthenware, decorated with an Indonesian shadow puppet in the centre; in brown slips on a yellow ground. Made at St Ives, about 1933.
Diameter 51.8cm./$20\frac{3}{8}$in. Mark: BL, in brown slip.
Collection: Crafts Study Centre, Bath

78
Vase, stoneware, with a speckled cream coloured glaze. Made at St Ives, about 1956.
Height 29.5cm./$11\frac{5}{8}$in.
Collection: Mrs A M Fernbach

79
Vase, stoneware, decorated with a geometric pattern of diagonal and vertical lines within horizontal bands; in buff on a mottled blue-grey ground. Made at St Ives, 1951.
Height 20cm./$7\frac{7}{8}$in. Mark: BL, block letters in rectangular seal; SI in circular seal; impressed.
Collection: Mr and Mrs Patrick Heron

80
Vase, stoneware, decorated with a geometric pattern of diagonal lines within horizontal bands; in shades of mottled brown and buff. Made at St Ives, 1951.
Height 24.7cm./$9\frac{3}{4}$in. Mark: BL, block letters in rectangular seal; SI, in circular seal; impressed.
Collection: Victoria & Albert Museum, London

81
Vase, stoneware, decorated with horizontal lines and diamond shapes in buff on a mottled brown ground. Made at St Ives, 1951.
Height 24.8cm./$9\frac{3}{4}$in. Mark: BL SI, impressed block letters in rectangular seals.
Collection: Victoria & Albert Museum, London

82*
Vase, stoneware, decorated with three 'Tree of Life' designs, incised, in brown on a speckled grey ground. Made at St Ives, about 1946.
Height 30.5cm./12in. Mark: BL SI, impressed block letters in rectangular seals.
Collection: York City Art Gallery

83*
Bowl, stoneware, decorated with a brown plant pattern on a speckled grey-green ground. Made at St Ives, 1945–50.
Diameter 23.5cm./$9\frac{1}{4}$in. Mark: BL, block letters in rectangular seal; SI, in circular seal; impressed.
Collection: Mr and Mrs George Wingfield Digby

84
Lidded jar, stoneware, with a dark blue-grey glaze and a tree design in rust on two sides. Made at St Ives, about 1956.
Height 16.5cm./$6\frac{1}{2}$in. Mark: BL SI, block letters in rectangular seals; ENGLAND, impressed.
Collection: Mrs Charlotte Bawden

85
Lidded jar, stoneware, with a speckled brown and grey glaze and wavy lines in two sides. Made at St Ives, about 1956.
Height 17cm./$6\frac{3}{4}$in. Mark: BL, block letters in rectangular seal; SI, in rectangular seal; ENGLAND, impressed.
Collection: Mrs Denise K and Miss Rosemary Wren

86
Vase, stoneware, with four flattened sides, two small handles and mottled dark blue and brown colouring. Made at St Ives, about 1956.
Height 29cm./$11\frac{3}{8}$in. Mark: BL, block letters in rectangular seal; SI, in circular seal; impressed.
Collection: York City Art Gallery

87
Pilgrim bottle, stoneware, with sgraffito decoration under a dark brown and rust tenmoku glaze. Made at St Ives, 1956.
Height 27.5cm./$10\frac{7}{8}$in.
Collection: Victoria & Albert Museum, London

88
Part of coffee set: coffee pot, hot-milk jug (not shown), sugar bowl and one of five cups, stoneware, with a speckled brown unglazed body, and the insides glazed with speckled grey. Made at St Ives, about 1956
Greatest height 15.5cm./$6\frac{1}{8}$in. Mark: BL, block letters in rectangular seals; SI, in circular seals; impressed.
Collection: Mr W A Ismay

89*
Jug, stoneware, decorated with sgraffito vertical lines and dashes coloured in brown and green on a grey and buff ground. Made at Onda, Japan, 1953.
Height 25cm./$9\frac{7}{8}$in.
Collection: Crafts Study Centre, Bath

90*
Vase, stoneware, with vertical bands of impressed decoration; with a mottled brown and yellow glaze. Made at St Ives, about 1955.
Height 35.5cm./14in. Mark: BL, block letters in rectangular seal; SI, in circular seal; impressed.
Collection: Victoria & Albert Museum, London

91
Vase, stoneware, decorated with brown leaves on a speckled grey ground. Made at St Ives, about 1958.
Height 33.8cm./$13\frac{3}{8}$in. Mark: BL, block letters in rectangular seal; SI, in circular seal; impressed.
Collection: Mrs Janet Leach

92
Bottle, stoneware, decorated on two sides with red 'tree' patterns with blue squares on a speckled buff ground. Made at St Ives, about 1957.

Height 20.5cm./8⅛in. Mark: BL SI, block letters in rectangular seals, impressed.
Private collection

93
Bottle, stoneware, dark brown tenmoku glaze with cut wavy lines on the side. Made at St Ives, about 1957.
Height 19.5cm./7⅝in. Mark: BL, block letters in rectangular seal; SI, in circular seal; impressed.
Collection: Mrs Gwendolen Mullins

94
Vase, stoneware, decorated with a band of lines around the top and cut curves on the sides; with a speckled brown-green glaze. Made at St Ives, about 1958.
Height 27.5cm./10⅞in. Mark: BL, block letters in rectangular seal; SI, in circular seal, ENGLAND; impressed.
Collection: Mr J M W Crowther

95★
Vase, stoneware, decorated with flower forms in white on a purple-brown ground. Made at St Ives, 1955.
Height 22.2cm./8¾in. Mark: BL, block letters in rectangular seal; SI, in circular seal; impressed.
Collection: Mr and Mrs George Wingfield Digby

96★
Pilgrim bottle, stoneware, with two small handles; decorated with an incised bird pattern on a speckled buff surface. Made at St Ives, about 1957.
Height 32.5cm./12¾in. Mark: BL, block letters in rectangular seal; SI, in circular seal; impressed.
Collection: Mrs Janet Leach

97
Vase, stoneware, with four flying-bird motifs in sgraffito and a cut line decoration around the neck; with a dark brown and rust tenmoku glaze. Made at St Ives, about 1960.
Height 33.5cm./13¼in. Mark: BL, block letters in rectangular seal; SI, in circular seal; impressed.
Collection: Mrs Pan Casson Henry

98
Plate, porcelain, decorated in the centre with a fish and a bird in shades of blue. Made at St Ives, about 1958.
Diameter 19.3cm./7⅝in. Mark: BL SI, incised.
Collection: Mr Michael Cardew

99
Plate, porcelain, decorated in the centre with a scene of fishermen in boats, in shades of blue. Made at St Ives, about 1958.
Diameter 19.5cm./7⅝in. Mark: BL SI, incised.
Collection: Miss Helen Pincombe

100
Lidded bowl, stoneware, with two small handles; with a dark brown and rust

tenmoku glaze. Made at St Ives, 1960.
Height 26cm./10¼in. Mark: BL SI, block letters in rectangular seals, ENGLAND, impressed.
Collection: Mr W A Ismay

101★
Vase, stoneware, with cut fluted sides and four small lugs near the neck; with a dark brown and rust tenmoku glaze. Made at St Ives, 1959.
Height 36.8cm./14½in. Mark: BL, block letters in rectangular seal; SI, in circular seal; impressed.
Collection: Victoria & Albert Museum, London

102★
Vase, stoneware, decorated on the top part with sgraffito tree patterns under a dark brown and rust tenmoku glaze. Made at St Ives, about 1957.
Height 34.3cm./13½in. Mark: BL, block letters in rectangular seal; SI, in circular seal; impressed.
Collection: Victoria & Albert Museum, London

103
Vase, stoneware, four-sided with a dark brown and rust tenmoku glaze. Made at St Ives, 1963.
Height 36.5cm./14⅜in. Mark: BL, block letters in rectangular seal; SI, in circular seal; impressed.
Collection: Mrs Janet Leach

104
Teapot, porcelain, with a very pale celadon glaze. Made at St Ives, 1963.
Height 12cm./4¾in. Mark: BL, block letters in rectangular seal; SI, in circular seal; impressed.
Collection: Mr and Mrs George Wingfield Digby

105
Vase, stoneware, decorated with a band of dark rust brown at the top, above a band of speckled grey with red patterning. Made at St Ives, about 1964.
Height 16cm./6¼in. Mark: BL, block letters in rectangular seal; SI, in circular seal; ENGLAND; impressed.
Collection: Mr J M W Crowther

106
Jug, stoneware, decorated with cut vertical lines; with a speckled yellow and brown ash glaze. Made at St Ives, 1966.
Height 30cm./11⅞in. Mark: BL, block letters in rectangular seal; SI, in circular seal; impressed.
Collection: Mr Henry Rothschild

107
Vase, porcelain, with a very pale celadon glaze. Made at St Ives, about 1966.
Height 23.5cm./9¼in. Mark: BL, block letters in rectangular seal; SI, in circular seal, impressed.
Collection: Mr and Mrs Alan Bowness

108★
Lidded jar, stoneware, with hexagonal cut sides and circular lid, with a dark brown and rust tenmoku glaze. Made at St Ives, about 1960.
Height 31.5cm./12⅜in. Mark: BL, block letters in rectangular seal; SI, in circular seal; impressed.
Collection: Mr and Mrs Alan Bowness

109★
Vase, stoneware, with four slightly flattened sides decorated with sgraffito tree patterns under a streaked yellow-brown glaze. Made at St Ives, about 1960
Height 23.5cm./9¼in. Mark: BL, incised; SI, in circular seal, impressed.
Collection: Mr Herman Rothschild

110
Dish, stoneware, decorated with an oriental pilgrim and mountain pattern in mottled rust and black glaze. Made at St Ives, 1965.
Diameter 36.7cm./14½in. Mark: BL, block letters in rectangular seal; SI, in circular seal; impressed.
Collection: Mrs Janet Leach

111
Two vases, stoneware, with cut sides and a streaked brown and black tenmoku glaze. Made at St Ives, 1966.
Height 43.2cm./17in. Mark: BL, block letters in rectangular seal; SI, in circular seal; impressed.
Collection: Cornwall County Council, Truro

112
Vase, stoneware, with wavy sgraffito decoration on the sides; with a dark brown and rust tenmoku glaze. Made at St Ives, about 1965.
Height 48.3cm./19in. Mark: BL, block letters in rectangular seal; SI, in circular seal; impressed.
Collection: Mr David Leach

113
Vase, stoneware, with cut sides, covered with a mottled green and dark brown glaze. Made at St Ives, about 1967.
Height 35cm./13¾in. Mark: BL, block letters in rectangular seal; SI, in circular seal; impressed.
Collection: Dartington Hall Trust

114★
Vase, stoneware, decorated on the sides with two sgraffito tree patterns on a streaked and speckled grey ground. Made at St Ives, 1969.
Height 42cm./16½in. Mark: BL, block letters in rectangular seal; SI, in circular seal; impressed.
Collection: Miss Kate Nicholson

115★
Dish, stoneware, decorated with a flying bird in the centre with a border of curved lines in buff on a mottled brown ground. Made at St Ives, 1966.

Diameter 36.5cm./$14\frac{3}{8}$in. Mark: BL, block letters in rectangular seal; SI, in circular seal; impressed.
Collection: Mr J M W Crowther

116
Lidded bowl, stoneware, with a curved conical lid, decorated with a buff sgraffito design on a streaked brown ground. Made at St Ives, about 1967.
Diameter 30.5cm./12in. Mark: BL, block letters in rectangular seal; SI, in circular seal; impressed.
Collection: Mr J M W Crowther

117
Plate, porcelain, decorated in the centre with a willow tree in sgraffito with pale blue and brown colouring. Made at St Ives, 1969.
Diameter 28.5cm./$11\frac{1}{4}$in. Mark: BL, block letters in rectangular seal; SI, in circular seal; impressed.
Collection: Mrs Janet Leach

118
Plate, porcelain, decorated in the centre with a flying bird in sgraffito with pale blue and brown colouring. Made at St Ives, 1969.
Diameter 28.5cm./$11\frac{1}{4}$in. Mark: BL, block letters in rectangular seal; SI, in circular seal; impressed.
Collection: the artist

119
Vase, porcelain, with cut fluted sides and a cream coloured surface. Made at St Ives, about 1967.
Height 28.5cm./$11\frac{1}{4}$in. Mark: BL, block letters in rectangular seal; SI, in circular seal; impressed.
Collection: Victoria & Albert Museum, London

120*
Lidded jug, stoneware, with cut sides and sunken lid; with metallic dark brown glaze. Made at St Ives, 1970.
Height 21cm./$8\frac{1}{4}$in. Mark: BL, block letters in rectangular seal; SI, in circular seal; impressed.
Collection: Mrs Janet Leach

121*
Vase, stoneware, decorated with vertical sgraffito lines and rows of raised pellets; with dark brown and rust tenmoku glaze. Made at St Ives, 1970.
Height 32.5cm./$12\frac{3}{4}$in. Mark: BL, block letters in rectangular seal; SI, in circular seal; impressed.
Collection: Penwith Gallery, St Ives

122
Dish, stoneware, decorated in the centre with an oriental mountain scene in rust and black. Made at St Ives, 1968.
Diameter 38cm./15in. Mark: BL, block letters in rectangular seal; SI, in circular seal; impressed.
Collection: Mrs Janet Leach.

123
Pilgrim bottle, stoneware, with white slip sgraffito and painted decoration. Made at St Ives, 1973.
Height 33cm./13in. Mark: BL, block letters in rectangular seal; SI, in circular seal; impressed.
Collection: Mr Henry Rothschild

Drawings and etchings

124
His Plot of Land, Hakone
Etching, 1912
Signed and dated Bernard Leach in plate
Plate 12.7 × 13.6cm./5 × $5\frac{3}{8}$in.
Collection: the artist

125
Temple of the Moon, Peking
Soft ground etching, 1916
Signed and dated Bernard Leach in plate
Plate 27.5 × 29.8cm./$10\frac{7}{8}$ × $11\frac{3}{4}$in.
Collection: the artist

126
Karuizawa, Raging Winds
Soft ground etching, 1913
Signed and dated Bernard Leach in pencil and in plate
Plate 15 × 20.2cm./$5\frac{7}{8}$ × 8in.
Collection: the artist

127
Bamboo and a Japanese Hut
Soft ground etching, 1914
Signed and dated BL in plate
Plate 15 × 15cm./$5\frac{7}{8}$ × $5\frac{7}{8}$in.
Collection: the artist

128
Hakone Lake, Japan
Soft ground etching, 1913
Signed Bernard Leach in pencil
Plate 24.8 × 25.2cm./$9\frac{3}{4}$ × $9\frac{7}{8}$in.
Collection: the artist

129
The Gate of Peking
Soft ground etching, 1918
Signed and dated Bernard Leach in plate
Plate 30.2 × 20cm./$11\frac{7}{8}$ × $7\frac{7}{8}$in.
Collection: the artist

130
Rocks and Moon, China
Lithograph, 1918
Signed and dated Bernard Leach in plate
Sheet 38 × 54.2cm./15 × $21\frac{3}{8}$in.
Collection: Mrs Charlotte Bawden

131
Fude, Iwa, Japan
Brush drawing in sepia ink, 1917
Signed and dated BL in ink
38.4 × 29cm./$15\frac{1}{8}$ × $11\frac{3}{8}$in.
Collection: Mr Guy Worsdell

132
Mountain Cottage, Japan
Brush drawing in sepia ink, 1917
Signed and dated BL in ink
29.3 × 37.5cm./$11\frac{1}{2}$ × $14\frac{3}{4}$in.
Collection: Mr and Mrs B H Bliss

133
Sleep in the Hills
Ink and wash drawing, 1918
Signed BL in ink
25.5 × 31.5cm./10 × $12\frac{3}{8}$in.
Collection: the artist

134
Mountain Stream, Japan
Ink, pen and wash drawing, 1919
Signed and dated Leach in pen
12.7 × 14.8cm./5 × $5\frac{7}{8}$in.
Collection: Miss Elizabeth Davison

135
South Downs, Ditchling
Pen and wash drawing in sepia ink, 1936
Signed and dated BHL and BL in ink
14.2 × 17.7cm./$5\frac{5}{8}$ × 7in.
Collection: the artist

136
South Downs, Ditchling
Pen and wash drawing in sepia ink, c.1936
Signed BL in ink
14.3 × 17cm./$5\frac{5}{8}$ × $6\frac{3}{4}$in.
Collection: the artist

137
North Cornish Coast, Gurnard's Head
Pen and wash drawing in sepia ink, 1956
14.2 × 17.2cm./$5\frac{5}{8}$ × $6\frac{3}{4}$in.
Collection: the artist

138
Gurnard's Head, North Cornwall
Pen and wash drawing in sepia ink, c.1956
14.2 × 19.3cm./$5\frac{5}{8}$ × $7\frac{5}{8}$in.
Collection: Mr Bruce and Mrs Monica Wightman

139
Page opening of a sketchbook
Pen drawings in sepia ink; used 1936–48
14 × 19cm./$5\frac{1}{2}$ × $7\frac{1}{2}$in.
Collection: the artist

140
Plate, Mountains and Trees Motif
Ink wash drawing, 1959
Signed BL in ink
31.2 × 33cm./$12\frac{1}{4}$ × 13in.
Collection: Mrs E M Younger

141
Flat Bottle Vase, Tree Motif
Stencil and brush drawing in ink wash, c.1958
Signed BL in ink
33 × 31.3cm./13 × $12\frac{3}{8}$in.
Collection: Mr Bruce and Mrs Monica Wightman

142
Flat Bottle Vase, Tree Motifs
Stencil and brush drawing in ink, 1957
Signed and dated BL in ink
34.4 × 24.3cm./$13\frac{1}{2}$ × $9\frac{5}{8}$in.
Private collection

143
Tall Bottle Vase, Bamboo Motif
Stencil and brush drawing in ink wash, 1958
Signed and dated BL in ink
45.3 × 30cm./$17\frac{7}{8}$ × $11\frac{7}{8}$in.
Collection: Mrs Barbara Cass

Select Bibliography

ARTS COUNCIL OF GREAT BRITAIN
Bernard Leach, fifty years a potter, London, Arts Council of G.B., 1961. Catalogue of a retrospective exhibition, introduction by J P Hodin, with 'Belief and Hope' essay by Bernard Leach

BARROW, T (editor)
Essays in Appreciation of Bernard Leach, special issue of the New Zealand Potter, Wellington, 1960. Nine contributors, including three essays and a chronology by Bernard Leach.

DIGBY, George Wingfield
The Work of the Modern Potter in England, London, John Murray, 1952
'The Art of Bernard Leach' in *Connoisseur Year Book*, London 1958
'Bernard Leach: fifty years a potter', in *Museums Journal*, No 60, January 1961

FARLEIGH, John (editor)
Fifteen Craftsmen on their Crafts, London, Sylvan Press, 1945

FLETCHER, John Gould
'Bernard Leach' in *Artwork*, Summer 1931

HODIN. J P
'Bernard Leach' in *The Studio*, vol 133, No 648, 1947
The Dilemma of Being Modern, London, Routledge and Kegan Paul, 1956

LEACH, Bernard
A Review, 1909–1914, Tokyo (privately printed), 1914
A Potter's Outlook, Handworkers' Pamphlet No 3, London, New Handworkers' Gallery, 1928
A Potter's Book, London, Faber and Faber, 1940 (2nd edition, 1945; 15th impression 1976) (introductions by Soetsu Yanagi and Michael Cardew)
Fifteen Craftsmen on their Crafts (edited by John Farleigh) contains chapter by B L, London, Sylvan Press, 1945
The Leach Pottery, 1920–1946, pamphlet associated with exhibition at the Berkeley Galleries, London, 1946
A Potter's Portfolio. A Selection of Fine Pots, London, Lund Humphries, 1951
A Potter in Japan, 1952–1954, London, Faber and Faber, 1960
Kenzan and his tradition: the lives and times of Koetsu, Sotatsu, Korin, and Kenzan, London, Faber and Faber, 1966
A Potter's Work (with introduction and biographical note by J P Hodin), London, Evelyn, Adams & Mackay Ltd, 1967, 2nd impression, 1974. Jupiter Books, 1977
The Unknown Craftsman (see under Yanagi, Soetsu)
Drawings, Verse, and Belief, London, Jupiter Books, 1973, 2nd edition, Jupiter Books, 1976
Hamada: Potter, Tokyo, New York, San Francisco, Kodansha, 1975
A Potter's Challenge, London, Souvenir Press: New York, E P Dutton, 1976
Beyond East and West: Memoirs, Portraits and Essays, London, Faber and Faber: New York, Watson-Guptill, 1978

MARSH, Ernest
'Bernard Leach, Potter' in *Apollo*, vol XXXVII, No 216, 1943

ROSE, Muriel
Artist Potters in England, London, Faber and Faber, 1st edition 1955, 2nd edition 1970

VICTORIA & ALBERT MUSEUM
The Art of Bernard Leach, London, Victoria & Albert Museum, 1977. Catalogue of a retrospective exhibition, foreword by Roy Strong, introduction by John Houston

WAKEFIELD, Hugh
'The Leach Tradition' in *Crafts*, No 6, 1974

YANAGI, Soetsu
Bernard Leach, Tokyo, Asahi Shimbun, 1966. Book designed by Hiromu Hara, with contributions by S Hamada and S Yanagi
The Unknown Craftsman, (Adapted by Bernard Leach), Tokyo, Kodansha, 1972

A Review 1909–1914 (1914)

I dedicate the following few pages to the seven friends who have most deeply influenced my life in Japan: M Takamura, K Tomimoto, K Nagahara, K Awashima, N Yamawaki, R Kishida and M Yanagi. With each I mentally shake hands. As friends with warmth, as representatives of present day Japanese art with respect, encouraging them to persevere and pass on their heritage to the next generation.

Preface

In the following pages I have roughly gathered together a collection of thoughts, most of them expressible only in words, which have come to me during the same period as that in which the other work in this my last exhibition in Japan was produced. I intend them as a literary supplement to it. A great many of them are transcribed from my diary, where I had written them down as suddenly clarified convictions. The result is that they have naturally formed a body of definitions. It is not my wish that they should be regarded in so precise a manner, but rather as the slowly forming personal convictions of an artist. Although they represent my present belief, I do not put them forward otherwise than as suggestions.

Introduction

Six years ago my friend, the artist Henry Lamb, asked me why I was going to Japan.

I was unable to give an answer which satisfied him.

Looking back however I do not for one moment regret the step. For not only must anyone who is free to build his own life always be ready to follow an idea which his best friends discourage, and which he himself may be unable to explain, but he may be quite sure that such faithful following of intuition, though it may lead him into unforeseen and even difficult positions, will yet both satisfy his inner needs and also provide him with sufficient material experience with which to build higher.

It is not enough for an artist to belong to the present, still less merely to reflect and repeat the past, however remote and exquisite, he must also be an innovator. Searching the past and present for his own soul he must build. All actions are the materialization of ideas, and the finest ideas are mysterious inspirations.

. . . .

Lafcadio Hearn awakened my childhood's memories of Japan besides desires for the strange and little known which I determined to satisfy by coming to the East. I came in the spirit in which he came, in the search for the strange and beautiful, determined to try to understand the life of the East.

After about two years I found that the art of old Japan had passed away with the old life and that that which lingered on not only lacked all vitality, but was also a hindrance to progress on new lines.

The realization of this caused me to abandon to some extent the exclusive study of ancient Eastern art and rather to concentrate my attention upon the western art which was claiming the entire attention of almost all vigorous Japanese artists.

This was additionally inevitable as I was at that time in no way adverse or bitter towards European life and art. Moreover although I had been to the best art-school in England I found I had not reached that stage of freedom which enables an artist to take part in the contemporary movements of European art as a whole, much less to plunge headlong into such an alien atmosphere as old Japanese and Chinese art.

Only now, after nearly six years, am I becoming ready to enjoy old Chinese and Japanese art with a feeling of security. During that time I have studied contemporary art through and with progressive Japanese artists.

Impressionism, Post-Impressionism and the later movements have come to me through their exhibitions and their friendship. I am grateful, for it has saved me from a great danger of being hopelessly lost in the pursuit of ideas, however beautiful, made for and by people of another epoch.

Another point gained is that the study of ancient art and craft which I have made, though limited, has been made from the right angle, that is from the point of view of living art – from the present. Now that I have reached the stage at which the enjoyment of the essence of a work of art is unhindered by its nationality I am going to leave Japan.

I do not think I shall return to work, but I hope to do so to China and India after some years in order to gain a wider and deeper grasp of the meeting and unification of East and West.

In the intervening years I hope to repay the debt I owe Japan by attempting to introduce contemporary Japanese art in London.

Life

The centre of Life is Spiritual Energy. (God)

The circumference is Material Energy. (Earth or Satan)

Neither exist alone.

Together they form Life, Existence or Reality.

Heaven is the control of material by spirit.

Hell is the subordination of spiritual to material energy.

Purgatory is the perpetual endeavour to harmonise these two.

A man whose life is guided by reason is in Hell, and he whose life is made up of one long strife between reason (material energy) and imagination (spiritual energy) is in Purgatory.

Heaven is reached with spiritual energy at the helm and physical energy at the oars.

Heaven is complete life – the marriage of soul and body.

Hell is incomplete life – the divorce of soul and body.

Every atom, drop of water, leaf, insect, animal, man is the outward form of spirit.

That which contains the greatest degree of spiritual and physical energy is high; that which contains the least degree is low.

That which contains the greatest degree in this world is man, and among men those of genius.

A genius is a man of abounding energy. He is the greatest exception. It is his work to alter the laws which govern the mass of mankind – the laws to which he is the greatest exception. The greatest geniuses provide new and better laws, the lesser destroy the old.

When we have learned to reverence genius we have learned to worship the greatest attribute of God – creation.

We speak of some people as being in touch with nature; this is the first requisite of an artist, and it means that the person who creates a work of art has the power, at least in moments, to reach down into the very soul or centre of nature.

This is also the most vital need of any man or woman and in terms of Christianity it is called 'the grace of God'.

In man God has retained the same law of spirit and matter, and he who by conscious creation carries out the Eternal Will must possess this power of reaching with his own spiritual energy to the Centre of Life.

This is the Christian truth that a man must possess 'the grace of God' in order to reach Heaven.

From the foregoing it will be seen that I believe that the man who creates is in Heaven and receives his own reward. I also believe this of any man who is faithful to his imagination or spiritual promptings. I also believe that all men have such promptings to varied degrees and that there is a possible Heaven for all men.

Art

Art is the organic expression of emotion.

Organic expression is a method or expression based upon the constructive laws of nature.

Emotion is produced when the spiritual energy of an individual forms a chord with the Central Spiritual Energy; this is brought about through physical energy, or matter, and further gives birth to love.

A great work of art is as stable and inevitable as a mountain or a tree or any other work of nature. In it beauty is inseparable from utility.

Beauty is external and internal, that is to say the spiritual energy of man requires the stimulus of external nature in order to conceive truth and beauty and to respond to the Central Spiritual Energy.
The surprise of beauty lies in the unexpected perception of latent reality. In the pursuit of truth and beauty, imagination must be the masculine principle and reason the feminine. In the neglect of this lies the chief curse of modern times.

Ugliness and sin are the children of misuse, they were born when reason first usurped the authority of instinct and imagination.

All nature is beautiful, but if we review the history of the evolution of life especially as it approaches its present apex, man, it is uniformly beautiful till the beginning of the reasoning power develops. After that there is a change. All things are beautiful and holy but all things do not contain the same measure of

Eternal Energy, some being more highly evolved than others. The value of an artist's conception depends upon his genius and on the divine or spiritual energy inherent in his subject.

The greatest subject in the world is the family group of three.

Art springs from life.

All primitive art is symbolic.

All contemporary art should be significant and synthetic.

The arts radiate from sex.

The sex characteristic were the origins of the first patterns.

Art was first employed as a decoration of sex.

Imagination is the synthesis of spiritual energy and accumulated sense experience.

The sex relation is the highest form of sense experience.

. . . .

I do not wish to paint what I see, but what I feel through the sense of sight and what I imagine. The matter of the profoundest interest to me is to discover *how* to organise the colour and form of objects so as to produce that feeling, so as to suit the material and space in hand, and yet preserve organic character. This *how* must be a credo of life as well as of art. Its component elements must be united by love.

. . . .

Y. asked me if I thought an artistic period in history was due to genius or circumstance. I replied that both were necessary. That potential genius must be present to be aroused by external necessity; this being the meaning of the English proverb: 'necessity is the mother of invention'.

The question reduced to its elements must be stated thus: 'Is life spiritual or physical?'

I believe that it is both, and that it is essentially impossible to conceive of a purely spiritual or a purely physical life. Buddhism is the philosophy of one and European Materialism of the other extreme. When Eastern Spirituality has united with Western Spirituality and Eastern practice with Western practice there will be born a new religion and a new life for the whole human race.

Consciousness

The history of consciousness is the history of the human race.

In the animal kingdom self-consciousness is that which separates man from brute.

The sub-conscious mind is a vast store-house of inherited experience.

From that treasure we take continually, instinct, intuition and inspiration; to it we add continuously.

Consciousness is organic understanding.

Self-consciousness is organic understanding of self.

Necessity originates habit which becomes unconsciousness, and inherited gives birth to intuition and personality. Intuition and personality obeyed, give action and experience, from which spring consciousness and idea. The man who governs his life by consciousness and idea is complete and can powerfully assist others.

The Zen meditations are an Eastern way of opening the store-house of the sub-conscious mind.

As the sun rises the dawn recedes across the western fields; as the consciousness of man increases his sub-conscious mind flies further afield.

. . . .

In youth the beginnings of self-consciousness mark the end of innocence and infancy, and in the Catholic Church this is arbitrarily fixed at seven years, when a child is first supposed to be able to commit mortal sin.

The beginning of self-consciousness, ugly though it may be, whether in the individual, the nation, the continent or the world as a whole, is the beginning of real life.

The last stage of self consciousness is self unconsciousness.

Education

Education is the awakening of latent ability.

This is accomplished by suggestion, by freedom and by opportunity.

A healthy psychological education on these lines has been evolved in Italy by Dr Maria Montessori for defective and ordinary children; is it yet too early to look for a natural and psychological system of developing artistic sensitiveness?

The present system of artistic education entirely crushes the naïveté and spontaneity of child art and folk art.

I attended the Slade School of art in London, the only nursery which has produced vigorous artists in modern England, but even there the system was hardly different from the ordinary educational method of instilling knowledge from without instead of awakening consciousness from within. It was always, 'action', 'construction' and 'proportion' and a complete avoidance of natural expression, feeling and imagination.

Natural education draws no distinction between joy and work.

Japan

Before East can meet West gifts must be interchanged.

The East is static, the West dynamic.

Future civilization will harmonise these two principles.

For fifty years Japan has absorbed the materialism of Europe, at the present moment her advanced thinkers are breasting the new wave of dynamic and synthetic thought which has recently inundated the West.

Europe has exploited the East but has scarcely begun to study its thought.

We await the meeting of these two movements, in the meantime let us exchange gifts.

The greatest need in Japan is of individualism, and to this end a natural and psychological educational system.

The art of old Japan vanished with the life of old Japan.

If a new Japanese life should be evolved, a new characteristic art will arise.

The artist who discards nationality must progress through individuality or self-consciousness.

The Japanese artist returning from Europe lives and works in the hope that his life as a Japanese has grown into something larger, his life as a citizen of the world, but in some cases this is a delusion. For in order to be able to call oneself a citizen of the world in this sense it is absolutely necessary to replace nationality by individuality and the artist who cannot stand alone in Europe as an artist upon his own merits is deluding himself if he thinks he can do so in Japan.

Fortunately I believe there are a few who can bear this test.

It is tragic to see Japan bowed down under the weight of the mechanical inventions of Europe.

Two hundred years ago the Japanese craftsman could take a foreign idea (Dutch) and blend it with his national ideas and produce a thing of beauty. Today he cannot.

Today he and his customers pursue ideas of European utility and misunderstood ideas of European beauty and the result is not organic.

Everywhere in Japan manual dexterity has become the criterion of the applied arts.

The disappearance of folk art under the pressure of commerce, which we can see clearly in Japan today, produces a general weakening of all sense of beauty in the common things of life and leads ultimately to the separation of art and the life of the people.

. . . .

I greatly regret that in Japan there is no permanent public exhibition of good European paintings by which the public might form a standard and which might help Japanese artists who cannot go to Europe.

It would be much more profitable if the money spent upon the Art-school and the yearly Mombisho exhibition was given to the making of such a collection, and artists were left free to make their own exhibitions, and the public to patronise what it honestly believed in, and not what the authorities prescribed.

Miscellany

The centre fire, the circumference earth.

Give according to your own and the receiver's capacity.
All know the Bread Law, but how many know the Law of Delight?
The lowest forever imitates the highest and deceives the middle.

We want dreams of the possible and actual for we must live them.
Art is a sensitive plant and withdraws at the least rude touch of commerce.

It is the true connoisseur who likes the quiet strong construction of a work of art, the public lights upon the salient points and neglects those silent corner stones.

Is he a patron who makes money by buying the works of living genius?

Nothing is ever lost.

The Chinese boat is derived from the fish, – eye – fin – tail.

The Chinese vase is derived from the female form, – head, neck, arms, hips, and feet.

You may take another man's ideas as much as you like if only you infuse into them enough of yourself.

See, the Devil in the eye of a snake
    all nature in the eye of an Ox,
        yourself in the eye of a Friend.

The wind pauses in her swift race, and the sun opens wide his awful eye when young Pyramus runs wild among the grasses with his wooden sword aloft.

The fire came and burnt up the leaves of grass on the hill side, and the roots groaned and said: 'we shall die, we shall die'. But in spring new leaves grew up stronger than ever.

The white road, a light breeze, and the common sun; from a house among the trees, room beyond room, a pure voice singing from the high alps into deeps of blue, cadence on cadence.

Moments when every dullest opposite face speaks a divine message, and the trees in the road wave like banners!

Is there not enough space in the world that men should be put in prisons? Is there not enough food in the world that so many should starve?

I hate people like B. I. who know all things, even the value of emotion, but have none.

Do you think the lovely purple grapes fear the wine-press?

Asama throws out rocks but the grass grows over them!

Artists paint their bodies and souls into their pictures.
. . . .

Impressionists, Cubists, Futurists,
Build your New Jerusalems:
They shall fall down,
And not a stone shall rest upon a stone,
But by one cubit shall the earth be raised.

There is some peace here, some domesticity, but I ache for the vital fires of living. We grown up lovers of the beautiful must burn ourselves if we are to see light. The child gazes fearlessly, round eyed.

Sap of the trees, essences of the air and of the earth fill the dry sockets of my eyes that I may see Life through a vale of tears. My heart is dried up and hangs like a root in a citadel of bones.

I should wish to take away men's breath with the wonder of my work, but instead they sit and smile and say it is beautiful! What have I to do with beauty? I want that plough-share force that cut worms hate and forgive, a share of that primitive energy which created the world.

Oh! the solid rocks in the shade,
And the running wind in the grass;
Oh! the square set house,
And the encircling garden;
Oh! the man and woman within;
Oh rest! oh action! together organic.

Out of calm night,
Over hushed fields,
Wrapped in grey shroudings,
Cold clammy mists,
Rises the light.

Crossing broad heaven
With footsteps so light
That birds alone waken
To welcome the sight
Gladly in song.

From the long valley
Rise the grey mists,
Float the sweet sounds,
Fades the long night,
Heralding day.

A Potter's Outlook (1928)

When it was first suggested to me in 1921 to write a personal statement with regard to my own work, I resented the idea, feeling that a potter's business was to get on with his job, and leave writing to those who make a profession of it. I was then fresh to the conditions of English Craftsmanship.

Having become a potter in Japan – a land new to industrialism – I did not realise the chasm which a century of factories had torn between ordinary life and hand crafts such as mine. I thought that, as in Japan, the work would speak for itself. But I have been forced to the conclusion that, except to the very few, this is not the case, and that unless the potter, weaver, wheelwright, or other craftsman, tells his own tale, no one else will or can do it for him. At this peculiar junction of two centuries nobody apparently is able to perceive the elementary conditions of our work, unless he has himself seriously tried to make some organically useful and beautiful article.

On my return to England after many years absence, the first thing that surprised me was the lack of any acknowledged classic standard of pottery. Out in the East this is the thread of life which runs through tradition. It once made a Japanese farmer say to me apologetically pointing to an ugly glass vase 'Please excuse that, I know it is not according to a Tea-Master's taste, but it pleases me'. It is only during the last few years that our archaeologists have discovered that we had a mediaeval pottery tradition with a form-sense equivalent to the contemporary architecture. An indigenous 17th and 18th century slipware is quite screened from our view by a hundred years of industry, although even here in the distant fields of Cornwall I have picked up many shards of the combed oven-dishes which were in use until 30 or 40 years ago: the name Wedgwood is still invoked as if he were a great artist instead of only the first and greatest of commercial potters. Even painters and sculptors are wildly ignorant of the elements of potting, and when confronted by pots are inclined to look only for such qualities as are aimed at in their own work, missing the beauty which is pressed, and thrown, and cut, and burned, and subtly devised to meet a daily need.

This confusion is depressing, for by it the thought is again and again forced upon us that nothing we could do, not even the production of veritable masterpieces, would receive the recognition which we all naturally crave, and without which, we can still less carry on than those in freer fields of art.

From this arises the questions: Who are we? What kind of person is the craftsman of our time? He is called individual, or artist – but how vague is the general understanding of the distinction even amongst educated people – and what is his relationship to the peasant, or to the industrial worker?

A moment's thought must make it clear that he is different from these, if only because he comes later in evolution. Factories have driven folk-art practically out of England, and it only survives in out of the way corners of Europe; and the artist-craftsman, since the day of William Morris, has been the chief means of reaction against the materialism of Industry. But, as a reaction, he has been almost as extreme as the thing against which he has reacted. Antagonism has resulted. The strife has been over the body of the public.

After 100 years, the trade offers us crockery which is cheap, standardised, thin, white, hard, and waterproof – good qualities all – but the shapes are wretched, the colours sharp and harsh, the decoration banal, and quality absent. There can be no two minds about it, if judgement is made from the level of the World's classics of pottery.

Let me mention a few such periods and sources: – Chinese T'ang, and Sung, and some Ming. Corean Celadons, Japanese Tea-Master's wares, early Persian, Peruvian, Hispano-Moresque, German Bellarmines, some Delft, and English Toft Dishes. Such pottery was a completely human expression, it had not been mechanised. But who has ever seen a factory-made pot with a nature of it's own – a soul? How should it have one, except it were breathed into it by the love of its maker?

Very well! What have the artist-potters been doing all this while? Working by hand to please ourselves as artists first, and therefore producing only limited and expensive pieces, we have been supported by collectors, purists, cranks, or 'arty' people, rather than by the normal man or woman. In so far we have tended ourselves to become abnormal, and consequently most of our pots have been still-born: they have not had the breath of reality in them: it has been a game.

I feel that we must be prepared to relinquish half our 'artist', 'art for art's sake', 'misunderstood', 'solitary', 'hand-made', 'hand-spun', 'hand-thrown', 'hand-anything' attitude, and come right down to solid earth and actual conditions, and leave our phantasy. I say 'half', for it is not a question of giving up that which is true in the 'artist' or the 'hand-made' attitude, but that which is false.

The next step is to get rid of the idea of the machine as an enemy. The machine is an extension of the tool; the tool of the hand; the hand of the brain; and it is only the *unfaithful* use of machinery which we can attack. It is here that Industry is to blame – just where it is unfaithful to *Life* in putting money values first. Science which has invented machinery in the XIX century, is no enemy of life, but 'business first' has turned it into a bully, a slave-driver, and a cheat. Art which is the outcome of and proof of life, must come into the firm again in the XX century as an equal partner, or there will be disaster.

Art has been a horrid 'veneer' in trade so far, but that is wrong, for beauty is an inherent demand of human nature, and work done without it is a starvation diet bound in the long run to produce disorder. The enjoyment of work for its own sake is what we individual craftsmen and women have to offer to an age which has mistaken the means for the end. It is this rather than shorter hours and longer pay which is at the root of our industrial unrest.

The widened demands of the increased population of the world make inevitable the mass-production of many utensils. It is good that machinery should stamp the iron of a railway track, or the glazed bricks of London Tubes – better than that it should be done by hand – plain, and clean, and strong and no nonsense about it! But that does not mean that labour should be employed eight hours a day, year in year out, upon mechanical work which gives no play to its creative faculties, for that is ROBOT work. With the increase of mass-production shorter hours are bound to come, and with them the time and energy for individual and home production with power supplied by electricity.

Granting then the need of industry and the function of the machine to reproduce with fidelity, the first necessity in pottery is obviously to reproduce good pots. This simply is not done. There are no commercial pots being made which can hold a candle to the classics I have mentioned for beauty. The merits which fall within the industrial scale are utilitarian and comparative, the larger historic, human, aesthetic values are unperceived. There are no hills on this horizon.

The pottery manager needs the collaboration of a man whose sense of fitness has not been crushed, a man who can design plates, cups, tea-pots, handles, spouts etc., in terms of clay and glaze with intimate knowledge of process. A knowledge that I can only describe as a sense of wholeness in which use and beauty find a new unity. He must enjoy each phase of the work himself and be able to convey that joy to his team. The work must become an end in itself and not a mere means to an end. He should know and really feel the rightness of the relationship between work, tool, and material which long ages had evolved before mechanisation came, and not just have run perfunctorily through a course in historic ornament. We have no evidence of the existence of such a man in the trade today. But in other crafts, such as printing, the thing has been done. In any case it can only be a question of time.

There is a chasm which urgently needs spanning, but before a useful bridge can be built there must be sounder foundations and a truer understanding between the business man, the scientist, and the artist-craftsman. Progressive firms have been working in this direction even in pottery, but it can be safely stated that nothing approaching the standard I have mentioned has been reached yet. Whichever side the initiative comes from first, matters little. Efforts from both sides are wanted – the factory needs quality, and we hand-workers must produce in greater quantity if we are to bring the prices of our pots down to a level at which our friends can purchase them for use. That is my essential point viz., that we free craftsmen must supply an actual need to a much greater extent than we have hitherto done. This will involve an element of restraint on the part of the potter-artist which will bring him in closer contact with life, and thereby provide a discerning public with pots in which utility and beauty are one. This business of going back as confederated purists to the hand which preceded the machine has served its purpose. The next step awaits us.

In Japan a small pottery such as mine would have a sort of family of half a dozen expert craftsmen each trained to a particular job from childhood in a very definite tradition. Two kinds of pots would be made, the 'bread and butter' pot, such as tea sets, sold at a moderate price, and pieces very carefully selected from each firing and correspondingly valued.

It is worth while noting in passing that the mental foot-binding which prevails in all these centres of traditional craft is a thing which has to be experienced to be believed. As long as that underlying spirit of race and place answers the slow change of circumstance the work done has national vitality, but when the barriers fall, and demand becomes suddenly international, and quite beyond the experience of the men in those work-shops, the springs dry up. Then a long time is bound to elapse before individual and conscious craftsmen emerge who can deal with the situation.

In Tokio I made shapes and patterns with the same enthusiasm as I spent on drawings and etchings, without thinking very much at first about utility and price. The pots were bought by people who looked, and were accustomed to looking, for the same essential qualities in handicraft as in so called pure art. By degrees I paid more attention to use, but it was only when I returned to England that I found, as in so many ways, an opposite tendency, a valuation as matter of course of the utilities first and the spirit second. It was impossible to continue here in so 'idealistic' a condition as to make just what I liked with only kiln and saggers as my limit.

The first daily-use pottery I was asked for was invariably a tea-set, but without the eastern teamwork, or our western machinery, the effort, especially at high temperature, is both back and heart-breaking. Making nothing else, I have calculated that by hard work I and a couple of apprentices could produce some 200 fifteen piece sets in a year, and we would have to sell them all at about £5 per set to keep going. I have often been asked why, given a good sample hand-made tea-pot, it cannot be reproduced indefinitely by machinery. In the first place your hand-made pot has to be translated into factory terms of devitalised clay, of plaster moulds, of unvarying thin fritted glazes, of coal-fed muffle kilns, and most of all, of men and girls who care so little for their dull jobs: the process is not faithful enough, not humanly comprehensive enough to reproduce living beauty. Secondly there is not the will on the part of the Industry. Thirdly, there is a chain of middlemen, with orders in their pockets, who have a fatal capacity for under-estimating latent public taste.

During my absence in the East I had become aware through books of our old English slipware, and one of my chief objects in returning was to permeate my work with its spirit. Since 1920, Hamada, Michael Cardew and I have revived the technique of the 17th century slipware potter. Cardew and I have tried moreover to provide sound hand-made pots sufficiently inexpensive for people of moderate means to take into daily use. But my own experience which culminated last year in an exhibition at the Three Shield's Gallery in Kensington, has taught me that however much this ware expressed the English national temperament of one or two hundred years ago, it does not fit in with modern life. Its earthy and homely nature belongs to the kitchen, the cottage, and the country. Many refuse it because it only harmonises with the whitewash, oak, iron, leather, and pewter of 'Old England' – moods which have been creatively 'worked out', however much I as an individual, or a few others, may have needed this experience as part of our personal growth. We cannot forego those other qualifications, of thinness, hardness, non-porosity, and light toned colour.

I then determined to see how far I could succeed in making semi-porcelaineous stoneware. I have reason for a belief that under favourable conditions it is possible to make household pottery with some of the qualities of the 'Sung' or 'Tang' wares of China. Such pots would satisfy the finer taste and the practical needs of today. The aesthetic perception of the modern French stoneware potter-artists since as far back as the 'eighties proves it. They, as usual, are in a much more advanced position with regard to their manufacturers, middlemen, and public than we are here. But there was a significant interest shown in their work during the recent Paris Exhibition by our trade potters: a leaven is at work. The gradual acceptance of eastern classic standards is an accomplished fact, and the museums of Europe and America have during the past twenty years set the periods of greatest achievement in Far Eastern art back by many centuries. These among other factors are producing an international public, not very large, but growing, which has a new classic conception of pottery. And it is chiefly

through its vague perception of our gropings towards a new synthesis that we individual potters exist.* Barriers of time and place have broken down and we craftsmen who have been named 'artist' have the whole world to draw upon for incentive beauty. It is struggle enough to keep one's head in this maelstrom, to live truly, and work sanely without that sustaining and restraining power of 'tradition' which guided all the yesterdays of applied art. Such nevertheless, as I see things, is our task and our privilege.

The outward changes I am making in my Pottery are very gradual, for any sudden alteration of equipment to a mechanical basis is out of the question. Each power driven device for saving monotonous human effort has to be tested not only, as in the industrial world, for efficiency, but also for what I have called its artistic faithfulness. An illustration may be useful: – In a Japanese pottery the impure cobalt ore which yields the lovely blues of old porcelain, is ground by hand for months on end by some old woman, who reads the paper, or chats, or sings to the quietly working painters. I have asked the latter repeatedly what difference there was between colour so ground and the same ore ground by power, and they have invariably said that the *'quality'* of the power-ground pigment for fine painting on porcelain was very inferior. It would seem that the microscopic granules of the hand-ground colour have greater variety, and that the tendency, as with the use of every new source of power, is towards abuse, or thoughtless over-use.

Actually, my first steps have been to begin with a change from wood to oil-firing, and from hand-grinding to power-grinding, and I shall not hesitate to put in an electrically-driven potter's wheel as soon as I can find a silent and efficient one. When it comes to the question of multiplying production, the complexity increases. I have not gone further than to have tiles made in quantity by semi-mechanical means, thereby halving the

price, and to devote the time saved in wood-cutting, grinding etc. to the reduplication of the more useful stoneware jugs, vases, bowls etc. by the old hand processes.

It may seem to some critics that craftsmen like myself can serve the most useful purpose, and incidentally be a great deal happier, by remaining free in our crafts, and not attempting tasks which they would probably describe as foredoomed to failure. Though they may be right as far as immediate success is concerned, I beg to differ. Instead I ask for support for a tentative and difficult undertaking.

---

* In my own case the problem has been circumstanced by my birth in China and education in England. I have naturally had the antipodes of culture to draw upon, and it was this which caused me to return to Japan where the meeting of East and West has gone furthest. Living among the younger men, emancipated from the shackles of the past, I have with them learned to lean forward in the faith of a binding together of those elements from the ends of the earth which are now welding the civilisation of the coming age. The potter, in his concepts, must possess such a sheer love of truth as will carry him past the dangers of revivalism on the one hand and of futurism on the other. With his elements of clay, water, fire and air he must, as long as he lives, strive fearlessly to clothe his vision in a garment of living beauty.

ACKNOWLEDGEMENTS
Lund Humphries Publishers Ltd wish to thank Mr Bernard Leach and the Victoria and
Albert Museum for their generous co-operation at all stages of the book's production;
the owners for permission to reproduce their pieces; and the following for permission
to reprint texts: BBC, London, extract from a broadcast talk on page 23; Kodansha
International Ltd, Tokyo, extracts from *Hamada-Potter* on pages 26–28 and 31 and from
The Unknown Craftsman on page 45; The Berkeley Galleries, London, extracts from
The Leach Pottery, 1920–46, on pages 29 and 32; Faber and Faber Ltd, London, extracts
from *A Potter's Book* on pages 33–35 and from *A Potter in Japan* on page 38; Souvenir
Press, London and E P Dutton, New York, extracts from *The Potter's Challenge* on
pages 39 and 40; Jupiter Books, London, poem from *Drawings, Verse and Belief* on page
41; New Zealand Potter, extract from *Essays in Appreciation of Bernard Leach* on page
44; Asahi Shimbun, Tokyo, extract from *Bernard Leach, The Man and His Works* on
page 45. Thanks are due also to Dr J.P.Hodin for his help, and to the following for
documentary photographs: Brian Seed (frontispiece), Andrew Lanyon (page 19),
Photopress (page 31), Mark Kauffman (page 34 top), Laura Gilpin (page 37),
Y.Nishitoba (page 42).